In
the Company of
Horses

In
the Company of
Horses

Kathleen
Lindley

Johnson Books / Boulder
Spring Creek Press / Estes Park

To my mother,

the late Sue Lindley Buesch Maki,

whose spirit I followed West

Published by Johnson Books, a Big Earth Publishing company,
3005 Center Green Drive, Suite 220, Boulder, Colorado 80301.
E-mail: book@bigearthpublishing.com
www.johnsonbooks.com

Cover design by Constance Bollen, cbgraphics
Text design and composition by Willems Marketing

9   8   7   6   5   4   3   2   1

Library of Congress Cataloging-in-Publication Data
    Lindley, Kathleen.
    In the company of horses: a year on the road with horseman, Mark Rashid / by
    Kathleen Lindley.
        p. cm.
    ISBN 1-55566-386-9
    1. Horses—Training. 2. Horses—Behavior. 3. Rashid, Mark. 4. Lindley, Kathleen. I. Title.
    SF287.L75 2006
    789.2—dc22
                            2006025751

Printed in the United States of America

Contents

Foreword
by Mark Rashid

I can remember the first time Kathleen Lindley and I met, just as if it happened yesterday. I had showed up at the venue the day before I was to begin a four-day clinic and I was introducing myself to the riders as they pulled in with their horses. I had met and exchanged small talk with three or four of the riders when a two-horse trailer pulled in. Two women began unloading their horses.

The first horse out of the trailer was a large chestnut quarter horse gelding. Before the second horse was unloaded, I made my way over to make my introduction. As we shook hands, Leslie, the owner of the quarter horse, mentioned she had enjoyed reading my books and said she was looking forward to the clinic.

When I reached out to shake the hand of the second woman, I got a somewhat surprising response.

"My name is Kathleen," the woman said, "and you know, to be honest, I don't know who you are, and I don't really care. But if you can fix this horse, I'll do anything you tell me to."

Little did I know that this inauspicious introduction would be the beginning of a journey neither one of us knew we were about to embark on.

It was clear from the start that Kathleen was struggling in her relationship with the horse she brought to the clinic, Ashcroft. It was also clear she had a strong desire to find a way to help things be better between the two of them. Mostly there was just something about her attitude that struck a chord with me right off the bat.

True to her word, she tried as hard as she could to do everything I suggested over the next four days. There was a slow but noticeable shift in both Kathleen's attitude toward Ashcroft and Ashcroft's attitude toward Kathleen during the clinic, and it wasn't long before the two of them were beginning to open a line of communication that had been missing up to that point.

I saw Kathleen and Ashcroft at one or two clinics a year for the next several years, and during that time something very exciting began to happen. Not only did the relationship between Kathleen and Ashcroft blossom and grow, but I also found that because the two of them progressed so much from one clinic to the next, it forced me to improve my understanding and ways of teaching—just to keep up with them!

As time went on, it became clear that Kathleen's dedication—along with the compassion and understanding she brought to her work with horses—was something very special. So special, in fact, that I eventually felt compelled to offer her a position as my full-time assistant, and that meant we would spend countless hours together on the road, providing horsemanship clinics all over the world.

Kathleen brought to her assistant's role the same compassion and dedication she had shown in her work with Ashcroft, and very quickly I watched her begin to evolve into a wonderful teacher and trainer in her own right.

In this book, *In the Company of Horses*, Kathleen chronicles some of the journeys, places, people, and of course, horses she experienced during our first year on the road and how those events are helping to shape the way she sees and works with horses today. She also gives us an inside look at the hard work, struggles, and triumphs she experienced, the long hours on the road, and the friends—both equine and human—she made along the way.

To me, *In the Company of Horses* is more than just a horse book. It's a testament to one woman's commitment to her life's work and the devotion that keeps her moving forward. Kathleen has been a superb student over the years ... admittedly not always the easiest student, but then the good ones never are. She has also been a fantastic teacher. And if the truth were known, I expect I have actually learned more from her over the years than she has from me.

To that end, I must say I am truly honored and humbled that she has chosen our time together as the subject for her first book, and I am looking forward to seeing what the future holds for this extremely talented lady.

I am also thankful for and very proud of the time the two of us spent together ... *in the company of horses.*

Preface

I stood in the middle of a big paddock in western Colorado, trying to learn how to catch my horse under the watchful eye of horseman Mark Rashid and a handful of clinic auditors. I'd arrived at the clinic two days earlier and had the audacity to tell Mark that I didn't know who he was, and I didn't care, as long as he could fix my horse. Well, something was getting fixed all right, and it wasn't the horse. The trouble I was having catching my horse, Ashcroft, was pretty indicative of our whole relationship—neither of us wanted much to do with the other.

I've lived, dreamed, and breathed horses all my life. When I was thirteen years old, I wrote an essay for school detailing how I was going to become a horse trainer when I grew up. My mother spent my college fund on horses and horse shows and talked herself into thinking that the horses and the horse shows were my college.

When I impatiently graduated from high school, I did indeed become a professional horse trainer. I trained hunter and jumper show horses in the Midwest for a few years until, at the age of 28, my life took an unexpected turn when I found myself in an emergency room after having a stroke, of all things. A blood clot had become lodged in my brain, paralyzing my left side. Recuperation was a grueling process. I learned to walk again, learned to operate my left hand again, and spent hours and hours struggling in occupational and physical therapy.

As soon as I was able to, I moved to Aspen, Colorado to be with my boyfriend and two uncles who lived there. It wasn't long after I moved to Colorado that I got the idea to buy a horse again. I suppose my real motivation was to prove that I could do it, ride and handle a horse, despite my handicap. Heck, I was still working on walking and opening milk cartons! I told my friends and family that I wanted a "resale project," a cheap horse that I could train for about six months and resell at a profit.

That's how I met Ashcroft. I saw an ad in an Aspen newspaper for a "sixteen-hand gray thoroughbred gelding, five years old" and figured he was worth a look. He was a sorry sight when I went to see him the first time. He was, indeed, a fabulous dapple gray, and additionally, he had very clean, beautiful legs and a nice head. But he was very thin, had tangles in his mane and tail, and was standing up to his ankles in muck, surrounded by a family of goats. When I rode him, I found that he didn't stop, didn't steer, and didn't go forward on cue, but he was willing to jump a railroad tie for me. I talked the seller down to $1,500 and took him home. I assumed this horse would fit right into my plans for a horse to resell—uneducated but pretty and well-bred.

Well, that was the first of many assumptions that Ashcroft shattered for me. Though I was a skilled horseperson and former professional trainer, I found myself out of my league with Ashcroft. He was easy to anger and would fight at the drop of a hat. He was fussy and high-strung. He was sick or hurt most of the time, wouldn't stay trained, and wouldn't be caught. I tried to sell him, but no one would buy him. If I got someone interested enough in him to do a vet check, he was lame when the vet showed up. I was stuck with him, and I hated it. I prayed he'd get hit by lightning, just so I wouldn't have to deal with him anymore.

After two years of frustration and fighting, I figured I had to do something drastic. I was out of patience and out of money, and I had nothing but a mess of a horse to show for it. I had heard that Mark Rashid was going to be in our area doing a clinic, and on impulse I signed up. It was a last-ditch effort on my part. That's how we ended up there that day, in that paddock, practicing catching.

Mark had caught Ashcroft a few times, and it was my turn to try. Mark suggested that I not expect Ashcroft to do all the work when I went to catch him; that it was plenty good enough if he just stood still and allowed himself to be caught. So I went out there, halter and lead rope looped over my arm, mainly hoping my horse wouldn't turn tail and run when he saw me.

Ashcroft was standing on the far side of the paddock, whinnying to some horses over on the other side of the property. I approached him from behind, as Mark had suggested. I saw Ashcroft's ears flick back to me occasionally, but his eyes stayed fixed on the other horses. I didn't know how the heck I was going to get him to turn around and face me, when he was focused on those horses. When I looked at Mark questioningly, he simply nodded and pointed at Ashcroft, encouraging me to keep at it.

I got to within about eight feet of Ashcroft's hindquarters, and I shifted off to one side so we could make eye contact. He whinnied again to the other horses. When he was done calling, I kissed to him, hoping he'd turn around and face me so I could halter him. But he didn't turn. I kissed again. And then he moved. To my utter consternation, he *backed up*, eyes still on the other horses, until his tail was within easy reach. I was about to kiss again, to ask for a turn, when Mark said, "You've got him, he's caught."

What was so shocking to me about this was that my horse had offered me what I wanted, but in a way I didn't expect. Therefore I didn't recognize it. This revelation begged the question, then, of how many times he'd done this during the previous two years of fighting and frustration. How many times had he offered what I wanted in a way that made perfect sense to him but not to me?

When I looked at the catching incident from his point of view, his actions made perfect sense. I wanted to catch him. He needed to keep his eyes on his friends across the way. So he accommodated both of us at the same time. Now, if Mark hadn't been there to stop me, I probably would have insisted that Ashcroft turn around to face me, because it's just not "respectful" to present one's hindquarter for catching. And that was the difference right there. It was why what I'd been doing with Ashcroft hadn't been working—I had failed to see things from his point of view. It had actually never occurred to me that it might be important to a horse that I be willing and able to see things from his point of view.

I took what I learned at that clinic seriously. I felt a profound change in me and in my horse, and I wanted more. I could feel the presence of a whole world out there that I'd previously been unaware of. I think there were two things in particular that led me to the change in attitude I was experiencing. One was the horse I had, who chose not to give up, not to kill me, and not to change who he was, and second, there was my mild handicap, which suggested to me that technique would only take me so far. I was going to have to think that all over carefully.

⋙⬧⬦⬧⬦⬧⬦⬤⬦⬧⬦⬧⬦⬧⬤⬧⬦⬤⋘

I've done a lot of thinking about my horsemanship since that first clinic with Mark. I've come to see my horsemanship as a journey—a journey with no destination, just a journey. I'll never know everything I want to know, and I'll never be as skilled as I'd like; there just won't be enough time.

My horsemanship is my life, and my life is my horsemanship. I can't tell where one ends and the other begins. What I bring to the horses is my life, and what I bring to my life is what I believe about horsemanship. If I need more patience with the horses, the place to practice patience is in the rest of my life; then I can take it to the horses. If I need to be more consistent with the horses, well, then I need to be more consistent in my life. Horsemanship is, for me, a practice, an art, a way of life, an abiding passion.

It's been almost eight years since Ashcroft and I first met Mark. Ashcroft's turned out to be a very nice horse, my muse and my mentor. Mark's been my mentor, too, exhibiting the patience of a saint and the wisdom of a sage, year after year. Teaching me was (and is) a difficult job, no doubt, but Mark has seen in me what I have not seen in myself. He believed I could do things I wasn't sure I could do.

After all those years studying with Mark, I'd perhaps become complacent in my horsemanship. My horse was going well, and I was moderately prominent in the small community of Mark's students. I was comfortable seeing Mark a couple times a year and then working on my own. My complacency was shattered when Mark invited me to become his full-time assistant/apprentice for fifteen months.

Being his assistant will entail going on the road, with Ashcroft, and learning to teach the horsemanship I've been thinking about for so many years. It will mean being away from home and shouldering new responsibilities. It will mean living my horsemanship more so than ever.

I realize I've been offered a once-in-a-lifetime opportunity, but I feel unequal to the task. Despite that, I accept, trusting that if Mark thinks I can do it, I probably can.

And so I embark on my own personal odyssey—a journey that will shape, define, and mold me, my life, and my horsemanship. I'll travel to places I've never been before, meet hundreds of horses and riders, discover my physical limits, and live with my horse twenty-four hours a day, seven days a week, something I've never done before. I'll be away from my home for extended periods of time. I'll be held accountable and responsible by someone I deeply respect. I'll spend fifteen months practicing my art and finding a path I can call my own.

When it's all said and done, I'm thinking I may not recognize myself.

POINT OF VIEW

Horses are fantastical creatures, all at once beautiful, powerful, funny, charming, and frightening. It seems sometimes that the very things we love about them are the things we begrudge them.

We love them for their power, yet it scares us. We want to borrow their physical freedom, while at the same time we strive to take it away. We know they're highly intelligent, but we treat them as if they were stupid. We expect them to read our minds, then deny what they find there. We praise their sensitivity, as we seek to desensitize them.

Our relationship with the horse is marked with fear, awe, love, passion, and of all things, contradiction.

I received the majority of my horse education in fairly conventional ways: at local riding-lesson establishments and then at hunter-jumper show barns. I accepted what I was taught as gospel and thought I saw it to be true. Looking back now, I can see the contradictions inherent in what I was taught.

I wanted my horse to move, to do athletic things, but I used equipment to hinder his movement. I knew my horse was smart enough to figure out how to open a gate latch, but didn't think he was smart enough to pick up the correct lead. I saw him gallop and play energetically in the pasture, but thought him lazy in his work. I spent so much time thinking about what he *wasn't* doing for me that I couldn't see what he *was* doing for me.

And that's how we tend to see it, or at least I sure used to; we tend to set ourselves against the horse before we even get started with our work. I'm beginning to think that one of the most common ways we horsemen do this is to not listen to what the horse has to say, or to misunderstand what he has to say, or to not let him finish what he has to say and put words in his mouth.

As I see it now, the horse is trying to communicate with us the best way

1

he can. And we're trying to communicate with him the best way we can. But we often (myself included) just have a tough time "hearing" our horses. In my own case, I was taught that horses didn't usually have anything to communicate, and if they did, they should stop it. Since I'd been taught that early on and had practiced and believed it for twenty-some-odd years, it was a hard thing for me to change. But change it I did, partly to reconcile those contradictions in my horsemanship and partly because the evidence I was gathering at Mark Rashid's clinics just didn't support my previous teaching.

One of the most interesting things we do at Mark's clinics is to try to help horse owners sort out what their horses might be saying and to help them see things from their horse's point of view. It's often not as easy as thinking a horse is being "bad" or being "disrespectful" and discouraging the behavior. Over time, I've begun to understand that if we can find the *source* of the behavior, the *why* behind it, we can reach deeper and more lasting solutions to the problems we want to work on. In order to do that, it is helpful to develop an ability to see the horse's behavior and what he's trying to say from *his* point of view.

For me personally, it's also been essential that I remove any emotion or prejudice from the situation. That's seeing something from someone else's point of view—seeing things for what they are from where they are, without prejudice.

Horses actually have a lot to say, I think. It might sound fanciful, and it might sound like anthropomorphizing, but horses obviously communicate with each other, so why wouldn't they try to communicate with us? Horses can't speak, though, and that's where we get a little hung up. We perhaps do one of the things I mentioned above. We don't think our horse has anything of value to communicate, we misinterpret what he's saying, or we don't let him finish his thought and then speak for him.

This desire the horse has to communicate with us is one of those things that we sometimes try to take away from him when we're working with him. I know when I was growing up with horses, I didn't really care why they did what they did (buck or throw their head, for instance); I just wanted them to stop it. These days, I wonder why a horse is spending all that energy on that kind of behavior, when he's a prey animal designed to conserve energy until it's needed in a flight situation. There's that contradiction again, and I have to try to make sense of it in whatever way I can.

Some people who participate in Mark's clinics are having trouble with their horses in one way or another. Mark will look at a horse and wonder what things look like from where the horse stands. If we can figure out how that horse sees what's going on, we can start to work *with* him instead of *against* him. If we can work *with* a horse, not only is it easier for all of us, but it also may allow the horse to retain the mystical qualities that we love him for.

Being Mark's assistant involves going on the road with him, helping out in any way that's needed (from being a map-reader to cleaning out the trailer), and teaching at the clinics. Clinic participants all get a session with Mark every day, and when their session with Mark is over, they can work with his assistant if they want.

For me, the idea behind being Mark's assistant is to continue to improve my own horsemanship and to reach a place where I can do some teaching on my own. It's one thing to be able to do things myself, but it's another to understand them well enough to teach them.

The work that Mark does has a lineage. Mark was taught by Walter Pruitt, and if Walter was taught by someone, then they're part of the lineage, too. But we can certainly say that this knowledge and philosophy was passed from Walter to Mark, and that now it's being passed to me (among others). That means that I carry a responsibility not to disgrace Mark (my teacher), Walter (his teacher), or the work itself in any way. That's a tall order, and it's pretty sobering to think that I have a responsibility to a man I've never met. But that's part of the job, to not disgrace the horses, the work, or those who have gone before.

So maybe the easy part of the job is doing the traveling and the clinicing. The difficult part is actually bringing dignity and honor to the work. I'm not sure I know what that looks like all the time, but it's definitely on my mind. Mark has often said that the more knowledge we have, the more responsibility we have, and I've thought about that a lot as I embark on this journey. More knowledge will only bring more responsibility, and I will have to be prepared for that.

My first trip as Mark's full-time assistant was in September of 2004, and it took us to Texas, just a day's drive from Mark's home base in Colorado. There were a couple of situations at that clinic where the horses were just trying to communicate something. Mark is very good at figuring out what horses are trying to say. He's much less fettered by previous teaching or prejudice than most of us, so it's pretty easy for him (comparatively, at least) to see things from the horse's point of view. It doesn't seem "insubordinate" to Mark for a horse to want to have a say in what happens to him.

One of the horses tended to hop and scoot while being ridden. Mark questioned the owner extensively about the horse's physical health, and she reported that the horse had a wreck with his previous owner and was developing arthritis in his hips, although at seven years old he was a youngish horse. A vet and an equine chiropractor had seen the horse, and they'd both diagnosed him with arthritis and a "dropped hip," but they said he was sound to ride.

As soon as the owner would mount this horse, he'd hop up with his back end and then scoot a bit, and he appeared tense, even after having been ridden for a while. On the ground, he appeared to be a quiet, kind, affectionate horse that had a good relationship with his owner. So I began to wonder what he was trying to say with all that hopping.

This horse also did a couple of other curious things. He stood still while being mounted, but he would tap one of his hind feet on the ground, as if trying to dislodge a fly. Only there were no flies. He also carried his tail off to one side.

We adjusted this horse's saddle so it fit better, and that actually made him worse. (*He* didn't think it was better!) But that made Mark think this horse might have a physical, not a training, problem. When we looked at all the horse's behavior, in context, that's where it led us. He asked the owner if he could examine the horse, and he found that the horse's hips were indeed the source of his problems under saddle.

Mark thought the horse might actually have a piece of his pelvis broken off. It looked like the point of his left hip (the ileum, to be more specific) was broken off and had relocated a couple inches below what should have been the point of his hip. If that were the case, it would explain his hopping under saddle. Perhaps he was trying to say, "It hurts back here, back *here!*"

As soon as she could after the clinic, the owner took her horse to an equine hospital for digital X-rays, which revealed a fracture of the point of the left hip, as Mark had guessed. To the owner's credit, she'd previously acted on the advice of a vet and a chiropractor, both of whom had unfortunately misdiagnosed his problem. To the horse's credit, he had continued to say he had a physical issue, but he didn't buck, he didn't toss his rider off, he didn't kill anyone. He just kept saying over and over that he had a problem, hoping that someday someone would figure it out.

So here was this horse that was willing to work as best he could even though he was in pain. That hop he was doing was not him being "bad," and it wasn't caused by a lack of training or understanding. It wasn't his fault, in other words. That hop, once I got to thinking about it, actually showed this horse's kindness and generosity. And maybe, just maybe, that's how he saw it too. Even though professionals had said this horse was okay, he was saying he wasn't.

I found out later that following the horse's diagnosis through digital X-rays, the owner gave the horse lots of care, including medical treatment, massage, and chiropractic help, and he was happy and sound for light trail riding. His owner was as much in love with the horse as ever, the last I heard.

———————

One of the other horses in Texas developed a problem with coming off the rail on the last day of the clinic. We were working in a big, clear-span, indoor arena that was set up as a dressage ring, with a short little white fence around the perimeter and the in-gate in the middle of one of the short sides. That gate led to an indoor stabling area. About halfway through his session, the horse began coming off the rail not far after he passed the gate. He did this insistently, and his rider corrected him every time. But despite her correction, he'd come off the rail again in the same place the next time around. She asked Mark how she might better correct the problem. He asked her why she thought he was doing it.

"I think he's trying to loop back around and go out the gate and back to his stall," she said. Now, this explanation didn't quite make sense, because he was coming off the rail after he'd passed the gate. If he were trying to leave the work area, it would have been easier for him to just go out the gate rather than go past it and loop back.

Mark recommended that the rider allow her horse to "finish his thought" by letting him turn off the rail and see where he wanted to go. That way, we'd all know what he was actually trying to do, instead of guessing and putting "words in his mouth."

When the rider let the horse turn off the rail, he did an extraordinary thing. He continued at the trot and made a big circle in the middle of the arena. So perhaps he was saying, "I'm happy to work for you, but can we do our work here?" In this case, it didn't really matter where he worked, so his rider finished up her ride in the area he'd chosen.

I'll never forget that. Here's this horse that's simply trying to ask if he can work in one area of the big arena, but his rider assumes he's coming off the rail because he's lazy. When I thought about it, I realized it was some previous teaching coming through. This woman had been taught, like me, that horses are lazy by nature and will try to get out of work if they can. In reality, he was happy to work.

As a rider, how many times do I interrupt my horse's thoughts and then finish his sentences? That's not only rude, but it also prevents any profitable communication between us. Come to think of it, how often do I interrupt people and finish their sentences?

Washington state is a good 1,200 miles from Mark's home. On the way there for a clinic, we planned for two days of driving, with a layover the first night in Idaho at the home of some of Mark's friends. I got to try my hand at driving the rig in Wyoming, where it is flat and straight. At fifty feet long, the rig is bigger than anything I've ever driven before, and the truck has a couple of extra gears, so the gears are very close together, which takes some getting used to.

In Wyoming, the snow fences are twelve feet tall and line the sides of I-80 for miles and miles. There's not a whole lot else out there, just snow fences. Mark says that I-80 is not a good place to be when it gets to snowing and blowing. The Oregon Trail goes through there too, and it's hard to imagine setting out across all that land in a wagon, camping each night within sight of the previous night's camp.

Mark's friends, Patty and Tim, live in Victor, Idaho, just over the Wyoming border. Victor's pretty small, small enough that if you're not paying attention, you miss it. Really. You can just about see the back side of the Tetons from Patty and Tim's place. They had a paddock all ready, and the horses were no doubt pretty relieved to get out of the trailer after nine hours on the road. Once they were fed and watered, Mark took a look at Tim's horse, which didn't like to be caught. He worked on that until dark, and we went to get fed and watered ourselves.

Mark and I planned to pull out again around 3 A.M. for the last leg of the trip to eastern Washington, where we were due for a pre-clinic demonstration at 3 P.M. I couldn't remember the last time I got up at 2:30 A.M., but my alarm woke me and within thirty minutes we had the trailer packed up, the horses loaded, and we were back on the road. At 3 A.M., you can get all kinds of interesting stuff on coast-to-coast AM radio, and we usually looked for programs about aliens and flying saucers.

I slept through most of Idaho and Montana while Mark did the driving. I was slated to do my first pre-clinic demonstration that night, and I've never been very keen on public speaking. I decided to wing it and figured it was just one more branch in the path I would be traveling over the next year.

Eastern Washington is an agricultural Mecca of sorts. Though it's a dry place, irrigation enables farmers to plant acres and acres of potatoes, onions, alfalfa, apples, buckwheat, and corn, among other things. Every morning I went on a jog on the farm roads between the fields, picked up stray onions missed by the harvesting machinery, and brought them back with me. Sandhill cranes flew over the farm every day.

While we were doing the clinic, I was overseeing an arena full of students and their horses while Mark helped one student in the barn area. While I was chatting with a student, Ashcroft kept turning his body away from the student's horse. I kept straightening him, so I could face the student as I spoke with her. When he'd left the arena, Mark had tied his horse, Mouse, to the arena fence. It finally occurred to me that Aschroft was turning in the direction of Mouse, and I figured that when I was done with my conversation, I'd let him "complete his thought" and see where it took us. Then at least I'd know for sure what he was saying.

When I was finished with my conversation, I dropped my reins and Ashcroft did indeed turn toward Mouse. He walked over, positioned himself right next to Mouse, and stood there quietly for a few minutes. When

I asked him to go back to work, away from Mouse, he willingly did so. He didn't try to go back to Mouse again that day.

So what was he trying to say? I still don't know, but I figure that for whatever reason, he just wanted to spend a moment with Mouse. In that particular situation, that was negotiable. We did what he wanted for a couple minutes, and then we went back to work.

I think that was the first time I'd actually thought about letting my horse finish what he had to say. I'd probably done it before, but not deliberately.

——◆——

In Washington, we saw another horse that had a lot to say about how things looked from where he stood. His owner, Jan, described Sierra as "easily distracted" and "not very responsive," which, when I thought about it, was a bit of a contradiction in that it takes sensitivity to be distracted and a lack of sensitivity to be unresponsive. So that was something I made note of.

Mark asked Jan to turn Sierra loose in the round pen so we could see what he'd do, and he exploded. He squealed, bucked, reared, and ran by himself in the round pen, with no encouragement from anyone. This went on for quite a while, until he was blowing hard and had worked up quite a sweat.

Mark began to ask Jan some questions about her horse's lifestyle. How much turnout did he get? How often was he ridden? What was he fed?

It turns out that Sierra was not ridden often but was fed sweet feed, supplements, and alfalfa. He was taking in a lot of calories in the form of carbohydrates, and they were providing him with much more energy than he could use in his everyday life. He was like a kid on a perpetual sugar high. All of a sudden his short attention span made sense. His other "misbehaviors" made sense. He just couldn't stand still, couldn't concentrate, and couldn't learn. And he couldn't help all that because of what he was fed.

For me, it's amazing how many of the problems we have with our horses aren't training problems at all. If a horse is fed too much food and has too much energy, that energy may well come out in ways we'd rather it didn't. If we try to train those feed-related issues out of the horse, that training probably won't stick because it's not a training issue we've got.

Mark recommended that Jan change Sierra's feed immediately to simple grass hay, so that we could see if there was any substantial change in his demeanor. He also recommended that she find some vitamin B1 to help him process the carbohydrates already in his system. Jan changed her horse's feed that day and got him some B1, and the very next morning we could see a big change in him. He was already quieter, and although he wasn't quiet enough for Jan to feel safe riding him, Mark did some work with him to show Jan how she could help him direct his energy.

This work was really interesting to me. Jan put Sierra in the round pen, and Mark took several objects and hung them on the metal panels of the pen. There were a couple of wound-up cotton ropes, a purple halter, and a water bottle on a string. What Mark wanted Sierra to do was touch each object with his nose.

Using just his body position and kissing noises, Mark encouraged Sierra to move toward one of the cotton ropes. The closer Sierra got to the rope, the less pressure Mark put on him. It was a lot like the game we used to play as kids where we'd help each other find an object by saying "warmer" or "colder" depending on how close the seeker was to the object. Once Sierra was standing with his head near the object, he naturally reached out his nose to sniff it. Mark backed away from him completely to tell him, "That's it!"

Mark and Sierra did this over and over with the different objects, and I was surprised how quickly Sierra learned first to look for the actual objects and, second, to touch them with his nose. After doing this exercise just three times, Sierra looked like he was asking, "Which one this time?"

Even though the job Mark had asked him to do was a small one, it was just enough to get him thinking and engaged with the world around him. Sierra couldn't have done the targeting exercise the first day, but as soon as some of that excess energy was out of his system, he was very capable of learning and paying attention. He became responsive instead of reactive.

That first day, Sierra looked like he had bugs crawling all over him, like he was uncomfortable in his own skin, as Mark would say. Is that what he was trying to communicate? When Mark asked Jan why she fed her horse all the things she did, she said that it was "traditional."

I think that's a pretty common reason why we horsemen do some of the things we do. We use a certain kind of equipment because it's traditional in our discipline, or we solve a certain problem a certain way because it's a traditional solution. I think that traditional tack, techniques, and ideas are great as long as they work, but I don't accept that just because something *is* traditional, it *will* work. From the horse's perspective, I don't think he cares how traditional, accepted, stylish, or expensive something is if it doesn't work for him.

After almost two weeks in Washington, we left for northern Oregon to do a clinic. We ended up at the foot of Mount Hood, which during our visit peeked out of the clouds exactly twice. For a while we thought the locals were having us on about there being a mountain there at all. I'd have liked to have visited Mount Saint Helens, since we were only about fifty miles south of her, but it would have been impossible to see anything through the cloud cover.

The stint in Oregon was cold. Really cold. We were lucky to have an indoor arena to work in, but it was still cold. It rained off and on, and the damp and cold soaked through any amount of clothing to the bone. No matter where we go, it seems that the locals say, "The weather's never like this here at this time of year."

Ashcroft and Mouse loved Oregon because they got to live in a thirteen-acre orchard-grass pasture, the likes of which neither of them had seen before. They get all kinds of different accommodations on the road—pens, dry lots, stalls, and pastures. They just seem to adjust and settle in without a lot of trouble. I'm in the same boat as the horses—I eat what I'm given, go where I'm told, and sleep in the bed I'm given (usually the host's guest room), which is kind of disconcerting after having been my own boss for three years. I've gone from having absolute autonomy to having virtually none, and it's something I didn't even think of as being part of the job. But it's a big part of the job.

In Oregon, we got to work with a couple of folks who jumped. One woman had been taught that she needed to apply her leg before each jump to make sure her horse would jump. Interestingly, her horse had developed a "stop" or refusal. The more leg she applied, the quicker her horse stopped in front of the jump, stopping quite violently sometimes. When I asked her why she put her leg on before the jumps, she said she did so in order to ensure that her horse would jump. I'd been taught this same thing years and years ago and had only recently begun to question it. Let's look at this from the horse's point of view.

The horse has been jumping for years. Once we turn toward a jump, he knows we're going to jump it. Why would I tell him over, and over, and over, and over, every step of the way to the obstacle, that we're going to jump it? Is he really that stupid? If he is going to jump a ditch in the pasture, does he need someone there, squeezing him with her legs in order for him to be able to jump it?

We're asking the horse to do something he can do by himself. If he has trouble doing it after we tack him up and get on him, what has changed? I wondered if (of all things), this rider's use of her leg was precisely what was causing her horse to stop. In her attempt to "help" her horse do something the horse could already do, was she actually getting in the way?

This rider had had a pretty nasty fall from her horse while they were jumping a few months back, so they really needed to get their confidence back. I set up a bunch of PVC ground poles for the rider and her horse to practice going over. I asked her to trot over a pole like she normally would, and her horse stopped at the pole. Then I asked her to replace her leg with regular, deliberate breathing. In and out, as many strides to each inhale and exhale as she could get. I asked her to point her horse at the pole she wanted to go over and just let her mare do it for her. I was thinking that her horse probably already knew how to do all this stuff, and if we could get out of her way, she'd just do it.

These non-traditional ideas still disconcert me. It shouldn't work, it shouldn't be that easy. Get out of the way, breathe, let your horse move and he will. It just can't be that easy, can it?

Well, this mare in Oregon just went around like a pro once her rider began breathing deliberately and took her leg off. She was smooth as silk and willing as anything. No stops, no tightness, no nerves. She trotted and then cantered all the poles like they weren't even there. In this case, I think the mare was trying to say, "Maybe the best way you can help me is not to help me but just to get out of the way."

⟫⟐⟪

In the tradition of horsemanship in which I was raised, what I'm now thinking might be true is tantamount to blasphemy. But I'm not just making this stuff up—the horses are showing it to me. I've really got to reconcile what I think and know with what I see. And what I see is that horses are, for the most part, the mystical, powerful, clever, hardworking animals we wish they were.

As much as we horsemen talk of "partnership" with our horses, I feel like we don't really want "partnership" in the true sense. We don't want to work with an equal, we want our "partner" to be subordinate. At least, that's how it looks to me, from where I am.

We call our horse a good "partner" as long as he does what we ask and as long as he allows us to hold the upper hand in the relationship. A horse that won't allow that is called "rank," "stubborn," "lazy," or "disrespectful." But I think that very same horse could be asking the rider to do better, to find a clearer way of explaining things, or to improve his horsemanship in some way.

At least, this is what's happened with me and Ashcroft. He still consistently requires that I improve my horsemanship; and once I make an improvement, he wouldn't think of letting me regress. If the horse is as fantastical as we say he is, then the idea that he might have something to show us about horsemanship shouldn't be that hard to accept. We already have the key to horsemanship in our pastures and have at our fingertips the best teacher we could wish for—the horse himself.

CREATIVITY 2

When I was a kid growing up and learning about horses, I never thought of riding or horsemanship as a "creative" endeavor. Writing stories and doing art projects for school were creative, but riding was like a sport, part physical prowess and part mastery of techniques. It was like volleyball, where I used my natural height and physical ability to get to the ball and then did drills to learn the techniques to influence the ball.

I did the same thing with my riding; I used my height and physical strength to handle the horses and did drills to learn the techniques that would allow me to influence them. I learned a whole lot of techniques in my many years of equestrian instruction. I figured that I needed to have enough techniques stored away that whatever situation might arise with a horse, I could refer to them and pull out the appropriate technique. I considered my horse knowledge an encyclopedia in my head. When a problem came up, I'd look it up in my encyclopedia and right there would be the answer.

That encyclopedia of techniques worked pretty well for me for quite a few years, until I had a stroke and became mildly physically limited, and until Ashcroft came along. Ashcroft looked at my encyclopedia and laughed. When I'd exhausted my supply of techniques on him, I had nothing left. I had no ability to be creative and make up solutions to our problems.

Since I'd never viewed horsemanship as a creative process, I didn't even think it would be okay if I made something up. I figured that being a good horseman meant being able to do what others more skilled than myself could do. I was constantly trying to fill someone else's shoes. I was never really myself when I was with the horses; I was forever trying to be as good as someone else. That might have been part of why Ashcroft had such a problem with me. I think Ashcroft wanted to see what *I* had to offer our relationship, not how proficiently I could regurgitate memorized techniques.

When I ended up with a horse that didn't respond to my encyclopedia of techniques, I had nowhere to go. I had nothing left to offer. I couldn't make it up.

Now I feel like horses are just too dynamic to fit into the narrow parameters defined by books full of techniques. I'm starting to think that maybe one of the marks of a good horseman is the ability to make up things as you go, to find a creative solution, and to be free of the prejudice that devotion to a technique can create. I keep coming back to how important it is to be able to look at each horse as an individual and to work with him accordingly.

⧳⬥⧳

After our first clinic with Mark, Ashcroft and I were on our own. I'd learned a lot about my horse and myself during those four days, but more importantly, I had a vague idea of what I needed to accomplish in order to get things to be better between us. I needed to show Ashcroft that I could be helpful to him and that I would listen to him when he had something to say. So that's what I set out to do. That meant that I was already outside the information stored in my encyclopedia. So I began to make it up, to do things that caused my friends to frown and local professionals to shake their heads.

To improve my relationship with Ashcroft, I ended up doing some pretty unorthodox things. The first thing I did was to ask the woman who took care of Ashcroft at the boarding ranch to leave him outside 24/7. Her custom was to have the horses out at night and in stalls during the day, out of the sun and bugs. But he never seemed like he wanted to come in and would pace and fuss in a stall, so I just decided to leave him out. We had to arrange for another horse to be out with him, since he wasn't comfortable out in a back pasture all by himself. Being left out there all alone would have caused him to have a bit of a meltdown.

Then I set about finding a food for him to eat that he actually liked. He'd been rejecting the ranch's sweet feed and beet pulp for about a year. I presented him with small amounts of different feeds, and he finally chose a mass-produced, pellet feed. He also refused to eat any feed with supplements in it, so I gave up the idea of feeding him any hoof or weight-gain supplements. He was fed the new pellets alone, and he ate well for the first time since I'd owned him.

We'd had a lot of fights in the arena at the boarding ranch, and it seemed like just *being* in the arena made us both tense. No matter how hard I tried, it seemed to set us up to fail and we'd end up in a fight. So I began riding Ashcroft in the pasture he lived in. I figured if he lived there quietly, he was more likely to ride there quietly. For a few months, I would mount Ashcroft at the barn and let him choose where to work. I'd just sit down and leave the reins on his neck, and invariably, he chose the pasture.

I think I was actually trying to protect Ashcroft from anything that might make him lose his mind. Now, life can't be like that forever, of course. But for us, for where we were at the time, I think I had to do that, if only so Ashcroft could see that I *knew* what was bothering him and I'd do what I could to help him. He had to know that I wouldn't just sit there and watch him suffer. How could he trust me and look to me for instructions if he thought I'd watch him suffer?

⊰⬥⊱

At that point in our relationship, I felt like I had to break a lot of the "rules" that I had in my encyclopedia. I'd been taught to never "let the horse have his way" and to certainly not cater to his every whim. I had been taught that horses should just do what they were told, whether they liked or trusted the person giving the instructions or not. But Ashcroft just wasn't willing to toe that line. I knew I had to show Ashcroft I was listening and that I meant him no harm. I couldn't figure out any other way to do it. So for better or worse, I made it up.

About a year later, something happened to Ashcroft that I couldn't protect him from—he cut his head near his left eye badly enough that it needed stitches. So I called the vet and sat morosely contemplating the fight to come. From the beginning, Ashcroft hadn't taken kindly to inconveniences like shoeing, shots, and flexion tests.

My most frequently used solution to these little problems was to twitch him. But due to my new focus, I really wanted to avoid the twitch if I could. To complicate matters, I knew that tranquilizers like Ace and Rompun made Ashcroft sweat profusely, and it was after dark on a cold winter evening. If we drugged him, I'd be there all night drying him off so he could go back outside with his friends. If I stalled him, he'd probably tear the barn down once the drugs wore off.

The vet arrived and took a look at the wound and confirmed that it did need stitches. I asked him if he'd be willing to do the stitches without a tranquilizer due to the complications. This poor vet had been underneath Ashcroft on some of his "unhappier" days, so I appreciated the fact that he was even willing to attempt it. As he got set up, I untied Ashcroft and hugged his head to my chest, saying to him in my mind, *Just do this one thing for me. It's time for a trade. I've cut you a lot of slack, now you cut me some.*

Within twenty minutes the stitches were done, with no fight, no drama, and no tranquilizers. All the vet could say was, "Whatever you're doing with him, keep it up."

I was finally cashing in on all the time I'd spent trying to help Ashcroft. I think he was, at last, starting to believe that I wouldn't make him suffer if I didn't have to. Furthermore, I think he was starting to believe that I wouldn't ask him to do something I knew he couldn't do, because I had, in fact, stopped asking him to do those things. So if I was asking him to do it, it must be possible.

⇒◈⇐

When Ashcroft and I were at that first clinic, I saw another kind of creativity at work, and that was in Mark's ability to see something Ashcroft did as a "try" on his part to do what I wanted. Specifically, when Ashcroft backed up to me when I asked him to be caught, that didn't look like being caught to me. But now I think that when he backed up, he was kind of like an artist painting an abstract painting. Just because what he came up with didn't look like what I thought it should didn't mean it wasn't a try on his part. In his mind, that's what catching looked like in that situation, but I wasn't creative enough to see it that way.

When a horse tries to do what we want, that try may not look like what we expect it to. It might be a little abstract. But if we miss that try, we won't have anything to build on. If we can get the horse to do something *close* to what we want, we can then shape that into exactly what we want—with a little creativity.

There's just no way to learn that kind of creativity from a book, and that's why it wasn't in my encyclopedia. I think the kind of creativity we need to work with horses comes from having an open and unprejudiced mind. It's a matter of being able to say, "Interesting. How can I turn that into what I want?" instead of, "That was wrong. Now do the right thing." There's just got to be a way to think outside the box, because I know the horse sure does.

For instance, at the facility in Loveland, Colorado where Mark holds his week-long clinics in the summers, there's a teeter-totter bridge. It's a wooden bridge that tips, so you can walk your horse up onto it from the tipped-down side, and after he passes the middle, it will tip down and he can walk off it. For horses who have never done a teeter-totter, it can be a bit disconcerting to have the bridge tip and stop supporting their weight for a moment.

There are a lot of ways to approach teaching a horse to walk over the teeter-totter. Most people use an "approach-and-retreat" technique where they lead the horse to the teeter-totter and ask him to put a foot on it and take it off again. Then they'll do two feet on, two feet off, three feet on, three feet off, until the whole horse is on the teeter-totter. The next step it to ask the horse to tip the bridge and hope for the best. But one summer Mark showed me that there's another way to do it. It's faster and easier on the horse, and it's creative.

Mark suggested that I walk my horse across the teeter-totter the "short" way, starting on the end that was resting on the ground. I could walk the horse back and forth across that end, working our way gradually toward the middle, where the bridge would eventually tip. But it will tip for the first time as the horse puts one foot on it and while his other three feet are still on solid ground. Most horses are willing to give it a try with their other feet so safe, and they'll push the bridge down with one foot. If they can do that once or twice, they often walk right across the "high" end of the teeter-totter, tipping it down as they go. Once that looks good, it's just a matter of walking over the teeter-totter the "long" way, the way it's intended to be done.

That little deal with the teeter-totter might not seem like genius, but I'd been working on the thing for two years with various horses before Mark got me thinking about it differently. I'd lacked the creativity to see the teeter-totter from the side. I just had it in my head that you walked over it from low side to high side, the long way. To approach it differently changed everything. My lack of creativity was what kept me from seeing another way.

Late night/early morning nationwide AM talk radio is something that I, having been asleep most late nights/early mornings of my life, hadn't known existed before I started working with Mark. I learned all about crop circles, flying saucers, and parallel dimensions from radio talk-show host Art Bell somewhere in Nevada, under a starry, moonlit sky at seventy-five miles per hour. We'd left Estes Park, Colorado bound for Half Moon Bay, California (south of San Francisco) earlier in the day, and after spending the daylight hours making our way through the bleak Wyoming landscape, the sun set over the mountains surrounding Salt Lake City, Utah. Our goal was to do twelve to thirteen hours, then rest the horses for a few hours, and be in San Francisco early the following afternoon to avoid rush hour.

It's not uncommon for us to be on the road for about eighteen hours. Mark's got a family at home, so every day spent traveling is a day away from his wife and kids. Mark travels as efficiently as he can—eating, fueling, and resting the horses all at the same time whenever possible. The horses get out of the trailer every twelve hours; otherwise they rest in the trailer during fuel/food stops.

On the east side of Elko, Nevada, we found a gravel parking lot for the horses between a neon-lit bar and a gas station. Mark parked the rig so that the horses would be sheltered from the wind by an earthen bank and sheltered from curious eyes by the trailer. We unloaded the horses, and I took them for a walk in the neon light of the bar. They shook themselves and blew their noses.

After six hours of sleep, we were back on the road. Rural Nevada at night was not much to look at, so we tuned in to Art Bell and heard all about how Bigfoot appears once in a while because he pops out of another dimension due to unpredictable fluctuations in the earth's magnetic fields.

I had checked the map as we made our way through the Sierras, and I knew that in order to get where we were going, we were going to have to go over the Bay Bridge, which even on the map looked like a very high, very long bridge spanning very deep water. Seeing as I'm just a bit spooky around deep water, I wasn't looking forward to that part of the trip. I got out an apple and ate it as we went over the bridge to give myself something to do, and it seemed to help.

I was struck by the pure density of humanity in San Francisco, especially compared to the barren, dry flats of Nevada, Utah, and Wyoming that we'd traversed only hours earlier. Little white houses blanketed the hillsides for as far as I could see. Midday traffic was heavy and sluggish. Had we hit the city at rush hour, we would have been crawling for hours and hours.

While Mark and I were working in California, I really devoted some serious thought to the idea of creativity in horsemanship, and I decided to use that word, "creativity," to explain what I was thinking about. I'd noticed that a lot of times, when people got stuck with their horses, as I had with Ashcroft, they just couldn't think their way out of it. And like me, their encyclopedia of techniques, by necessity, eventually ran out.

In Half Moon Bay, we met Nancy and her horse, both of whom had worked with Mark the previous year. At this clinic, Nancy wanted to work on transitions because her horse had been bucking or kicking out whenever she asked for the canter. Nancy had been advised by a couple of different trainers to sit down and ask harder with her leg to discourage the buck. Mark had Nancy show him the transition, and sure enough, her horse did pop up his hind end as she asked for the canter.

I was interested to see what approach Mark would take with Nancy, because I sensed a creative solution from him in the works. Mark asked Nancy to first try cutting her cue for the canter in half just to see what happened. The next transition was better and still plenty energetic, so Mark suggested Nancy cut her cue in half again. After about fifteen minutes, Nancy had cut her canter cue all the way down to an exhale. The timing of the breath was the key. As long as Nancy exhaled as her horse's outside hind foot was coming off the ground (effectively telling that foot to pick up the canter as it landed), her horse quietly cantered off on the correct lead. Her horse stopped all his bucking and kicking and just cheerfully made the transition.

To me, that was a really creative solution to a fairly typical problem horsemen might call "resistance to the aids" or something like that. Mark's solution was just the opposite of what I had in my personal encyclopedia and what Nancy had been told to do. Like her, I'd been taught to increase the intensity or pressure of the aid to discourage the resistance. Mark's approach was to see if the horse was resisting because the cue was just too much. And if reducing the cue hadn't worked, Mark would have just changed direction to find something that did work. Mark didn't really care what the solution was in the end, and he was willing to make stuff up until something clicked.

When I got to thinking about Nancy and her canter transitions later that night, it occurred to me that I hadn't just learned yet another technique to add to my encyclopedia. What I'd learned was that I wanted to have the courage and the creativity to think like Mark did, to invent solutions based on what I knew about horses. After all, wasn't it obvious? Nancy knew she wanted to canter. Her horse knew how to canter, and he knew what the cue to canter was. He was also capable of feeling a fly sitting on the hair of his coat. So why not try going lighter with the cue instead of heavier?

Why not? Simply because that's not what we've been taught.

⎯⎯⎯⎯⎯⎯⎯

After a clinic in Moss Beach, California, we trekked down the Pacific Coast Highway to Arroyo Grande, where Mark was scheduled for another four-day clinic. And it was during that clinic that I got to put my thoughts about creativity to the test. Part of my job with Mark was to jump right in and teach. After their hour working with Mark, many students continued their work with me. I answered questions and helped people practice what they'd started with Mark.

In Arroyo Grande, I began to help a woman who was working on turns on the forehand and turns on the haunches. Her horse was fairly green, and she hadn't quite known how to approach lateral work, so that day at the clinic was really the first time they'd done it. Their turn on the forehand was going well. That turn tends to be the less difficult one since the horse naturally carries more of his weight on his front end, making it easier for him to move his hind end around his front end.

However, to execute the turn on the haunches, the horse has to transfer extra weight to his hindquarters in order to move his front end around his hind end. For a green horse that can be a bit confusing, as well as physically difficult. Usually, if we ask the horse to rock back or even take a step or two back, he will bring his front end right around with just a light neck rein. As I watched the horse and rider working on the turn, I realized this little horse just wasn't getting it.

I thought about getting off my horse to push on the horse's shoulder, but I didn't want them to become dependent on a third party to be able to do the turn. It was time for me to be creative and make something up that would help this rider and her horse out of this little bind before somebody got frustrated.

The rider and her horse had plenty of "forward," in that they had a nice walk, even though we'd been backing up for a while trying to get the turn on the haunches. So I thought maybe we could start there, since the walk was working. I wondered what would happen if the horse was walking and the rider then asked for a ninety-degree turn by bringing the horse's front end around with the turn-on-the-haunches cue. I suggested the rider give it a try, and the young horse walked a nice corner by moving her front end. They did a few of those, and then I asked the rider to "take the walk out of the turn," so that she was basically walking into a turn on the haunches. It worked! After practicing that for a bit, the rider asked for the turn on the haunches at a standstill. The horse had no problem. Maybe I shouldn't have been surprised, but I was.

I thought that walking into the turn on the haunches would put the horse on his forehand, making it impossible for him to pivot around the hindquarters. But that's not what happened. When I reflect on it, finding the solution to this problem was not that difficult, but it was scary just to make something up. My encyclopedia had run out, and the knowledge I'd received from Mark himself had run out. So I made a guess. It's like guessing on a test in school, in that they say you're best off sticking with your first guess. I stuck with my first guess and it turned out okay.

I know that I spent a lot of time trying to do my horse work the way other people do theirs. The way they do their horse work may be good for them, but it may be the last thing I need to be doing. It takes a lot of courage and confidence to "make it up" and look at things from our own perspective. But I believe that until I start practicing my own horsemanship instead of someone else's, I won't really know who I am as a horseman. I've spent a lot of time looking at the way other people work with horses, and maybe that's actually distracted me from looking at the way I work with horses. As long as I'm trying to be someone else, I can't be *me*. And the horses know that.

A lot of us horsemen, even beginning or inexperienced ones, have a "little voice" inside us that comes up with ideas, asks questions, or even gives warnings, but we get to analyzing that little voice or listening to our friends or those allegedly wiser than us and our little voice goes out the window. I wonder if that voice isn't our own instinct at work. Maybe creativity is there for all of us, and it's just a matter of having the guts to exercise it. Perhaps one of the things that separates us from those master horsemen out there is their ability to listen to that "little voice" and capitalize upon it.

Horses are creative creatures. They're intuitive and sensitive, and if they want to do something badly enough, they'll figure out a way to get it done. Maybe it's that creativity in them that gets the best of us sometimes and leaves us feeling manipulated or taken advantage of, which we're not, of course. Those creative things horses do are just horses being horses. Instead of trying to stamp that creativity out of them, we could look at it and learn from it instead.

I think we horsemen spend a lot of time trying to get horses to think like people. But horses can't think like people. I'm not sure they'd want to anyway. Maybe in order to work with a horse—who is just what he is, a horse—we need to be as much like him as possible.

If we can think like a horse, see like him, hear like him, breathe like him, and move like him, then aren't we most of the way toward achieving that mystical oneness that we're looking for?

PRACTICE 3

From as early as I can remember, all I've ever wanted to be is a horse trainer. I've dreamed and breathed horses since *before* I can remember. I've loved everything about them—the smell of their sweat, the feel of their velvet noses, the sound of their breathing, and the sight of all that power. When I was a kid, I confided all my secrets to the horses, knowing they'd never betray me. As an adult, I sought to borrow my horse's sound body to replace my own damaged one, if only for a while. With the horses, I found justice and peace and wholeness.

When I began riding with Mark in 1997, I wasn't really looking to learn more about horses or horsemanship. I just needed someone to fix my horse so I could sell him as I'd planned. I had thought of myself as a pretty skilled horseman for quite a few years. I'd won a bunch of stuff at horse shows all over the Midwest, and then I'd been a successful trainer and won more stuff doing that. So I was thinking that I'd pretty much "arrived." I was proficient at what I did, and I had the ribbons to prove it. Sure, my stroke had thrown a bit of a monkey wrench into the works, but even so, I felt I'd pretty much finished my equestrian education and was coasting.

One of the many things that Mark showed me at that first clinic in 1997 was that there can be many layers to horsemanship. I hadn't really thought about it that way. I'd thought of horsemanship like a skill set or a collection of knowledge or proficiency at techniques. When I began to understand what Mark was trying to show me, I started to see the possibility of the endless journey, the destinationless trip that is horsemanship to some, Mark among them.

Now I like to think of my horsemanship as having layers, like an onion. You can peel off one layer only to find another underneath. And

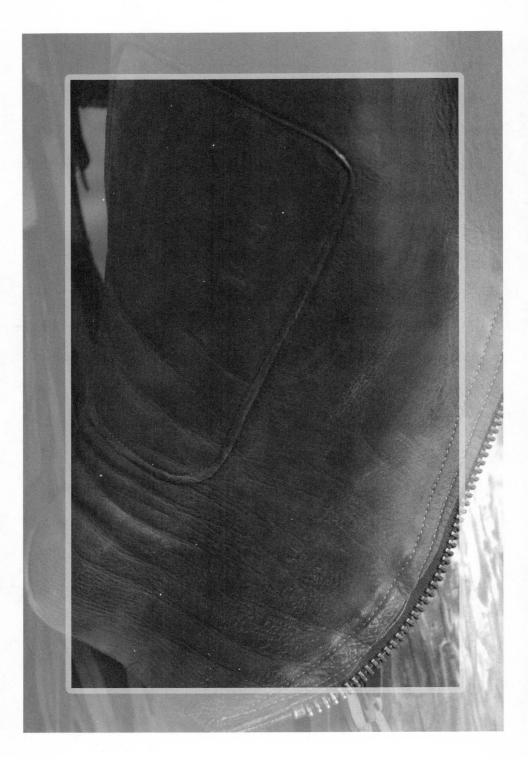

then another under that and another under that. For instance, where consistency is concerned, one way I can be consistent is to ride the same, four days a week, every week. That's one layer of consistency. I can back my horse out of my space every time he enters it uninvited, and that's another layer of consistency. And then I can back my horse out of my space even when I'm talking to someone and my horse is in my peripheral vision. That's another layer of consistency. When I get one layer of consistency mastered, it's time to find the next layer.

Or take the trot, for instance. A trot was just a trot to me for a long time. But Mark helped me see that under that two-beat gait are a lot of other layers. Is it fast, slow, tight, relaxed? Is my horse breathing? Is he breathing rhythmically? How far under him are his hind feet reaching? Is he soft and connected front-to-back or is he tight and disconnected? Is he heavy in front? What do his feet sound like when they hit the ground? And under all those things are other things I may not even be able to imagine yet. The same applies for everything else in my horsemanship, things like timing, awareness, feel, sensitivity, and concentration. Once I get something about as good as I can get it, it's time to peel off another layer and start over.

My job as a serious student of horsemanship—and especially as Mark's assistant—is to peel my onion. It doesn't matter how long it takes or what it looks like while I'm doing it, it just matters that I keep peeling. And I can live with that, as it allows me to never have to be perfect, only better than yesterday. That's not a bad way to be, and it's a lot easier than trying to reach some imaginary "destination" in my horsemanship.

Because horses are the way they are, if we're serious about our horsemanship, I think that we end up *living* our horsemanship. Mark calls this idea "horsemanship through life." He's been talking about it at his clinics for a few years now and has written a book with that as the title. As an example of this concept, if we find we're not very patient with our horse, we're probably not very patient in the rest of our lives. If we are perhaps really good at sensing a horse's needs, we're probably pretty good at sensing the needs of the people around us.

Horses have a funny way of exposing the areas in our lives that need work, and I don't think that they buy it when we live our lives one way and act another when we're around them. I think they can see that coming a mile off, and they don't like it.

When I began working for Mark, I sometimes heard him say, "How we practice is how we'll go." I thought about that a lot as I did my work. I think in part he meant that we can't, say, live our lives in turmoil and then expect to be calm and thoughtful around our horses. We can't expect to bring to our horses the skills and qualities of character that we don't practice in everyday life. If that's true, maybe the time and place to practice our horsemanship is not just in the two hours we're with the horses, it's also in the twenty-two hours of that day that we're not.

As I traveled with Mark, as we worked and laughed and ate together, I began to see that Mark really *did* practice his horsemanship all the time. He was the same person driving the truck as he was working during a clinic. He was the same person telling a joke at dinner as he was working during a clinic. The more time I spent working with Mark, the more I could see what the horses saw in him: consistency, even-temperedness, and trustworthiness. Mark wasn't putting on an act for the horses, that's just the way he lives. So by the time he gets to the horses, he's got all that stuff going in his life already. That really got me thinking.

"How we practice is how we'll go." Under stress, I'll revert to what I practice most. If I practice being frustrated in my everyday life, I'll probably find frustration to be a default of sorts in my horsemanship. It's what I practice and what I know. Or if I practice interrupting people when they're talking to me when I'm away from the horses, I'll probably interrupt horses and human students as well. What I practice most will come most easily to me, for better or worse.

The other aspect of "practice" that I began to think about was the kind of practice that a doctor or a lawyer has, or a veterinarian, or even a martial artist. The thing about all of them is that wherever they are, whatever they're doing, they're still a doctor, a lawyer, a vet, or a martial artist. If a doctor is golfing on a Saturday and his golfing partner has a heart attack, he will practice medicine right then and there. That's who he is and what he does.

It's the same with a lawyer. He will always be asked legal questions at parties. That's who he is. If a vet sees a dog get hit by a car, he will stop to practice veterinary medicine on the side of the road. If a martial artist is attacked on the street beside an ATM, he will practice his art and defend himself. In each case, these people practice their art at every opportunity; it's just what they do.

After starting my job with Mark, I decided that in order for me to be able to do the job I wanted to do—helping people with their horses—I would try to live each moment the way I wanted to be while I was doing that job. I would try to go through my life the way I wanted to go through my job. I would try to be, everywhere, the way I wanted to be when I was with the horses. Then perhaps that justice, peace, and wholeness I found when I was with the horses would come from me, and I could take it with me wherever I went.

In January of 2005, I flew with Mark to the United Kingdom, where he was booked to do three clinics, two in England and one in Scotland. In England, unlike in America, I could see and feel the vestiges of their horse culture as it once was. Giant figures of horses are carved into ancient chalk hillsides; paths through towns and villages are designated solely for horses; Horse and Hound *magazine is printed weekly and available at supermarkets; and even the smallest towns have a tack shop.*

It seems there isn't a part of the country that hasn't been trod on by horses or ponies at some point in time. And that horse culture is still alive. British horse owners are enthusiastic, well-educated, and hungry for more information. This place, I thought, with its horse culture and its people, is where I would immerse myself in the practice of horsemanship.

When Mark goes overseas, he does not take horses with him. That may seem like a silly thing to mention, but people here in America always ask that question. The trip to England was my first time out of the country since I was a baby, so I was pretty excited to get to go.

In order to keep things affordable for everyone, we flew "Economy Plus," which was basically between first class and coach. Our seats were the same as those in coach, but we had about six inches of extra legroom. Since both of us are pretty tall, those six inches were the difference between nine hours of misery and nine hours of sleep. Mark had told me that the best way to deal with the impending jet lag we would experience was to sleep as much as possible on the plane, stay up the next day no matter what, and go to bed at what would be "normal" time according to the U.K. clock.

To that end, after we got in at Heathrow, we collected our baggage, met our U.K. sponsor, and went off on a sightseeing jaunt. We had lunch at a "tea room" in a small village, where I learned a lot about mealtime etiquette in the U.K. I learned that when you drink tea, you never put the sugar or milk (what's up with that, anyway?) in the cup before the tea. You always put the tea in your cup first. I also figured out that you always eat with a knife and a fork, with the knife held in the right hand and the fork (tines down, always) in the left. This took a lot of practice, as I was accustomed to eating right-handed and to using my fork like a shovel, which is certainly not "continental."

The British eat everything with a knife and fork held this way, even things like peas. I asked a lot of questions and decided to practice using my knife and fork like the British do, even though our sponsor said it wouldn't be rude to use our utensils the American way.

Next, we took a walk through Avebury, which is an ancient town with a large stone circle in it. Some people say that Avebury is a better example of the stone circle than Stonehenge, but not having seen Stonehenge, I couldn't say. The town was lovely and very "English" to my inexperienced eyes, with narrow streets and a gorgeous old church. The stone circle was fascinating and had a deep dike around it. I decided I'd put some English history on my reading list so I could appreciate it all better.

While we were in the U.K. I decided to pick two things to practice in my horsemanship, and then I'd see how consistent I could be in that practice. I would look for every opportunity, inside the arena or outside of it, to work on them. The two things I chose to practice were my *focus* and my *awareness*. Mark often talks to students about them, and I felt they were good things for me to work on as well.

"Focus" is my ability to give what I'm doing my full attention, to finish what I start, and to keep track of what I'm trying to accomplish. This may sound rudimentary, but for me, it's not. I've spent many hours on horseback planning the rest of my day or thinking about something other than what I was doing with my horse. That's a lack of focus. While I'm riding my horse, I should be thinking about riding my horse, because if I'm checked out and my horse happens to check out, *no one* is home, so to speak, and that's a recipe for disaster.

I have also lacked focus in that I've often lost track of what I was trying to accomplish with my horse. For instance, I've wanted to work on bringing my horse on the bit at the trot and, while doing that, noticed that he's cutting the corners of the arena. So I've started working on that, and noticed that his stride has shortened and he's lost his impulsion. So I've started working on that. I have often ended up so far from what I wanted to work on in the first place that a training session has turned into a muddle of various half-finished things. If I'm working on a particular thing, I need to be able to focus on that and finish it before moving on.

"Awareness" is my ability to use my senses to gather information and my ability to be consistently attentive to my horse, my student, their horse, and the surroundings. In order to do good work with horses, I need to be aware of everything that I can, but not distracted by those same things. Awareness is another one of those things that has many layers, like an onion.

Mark's awareness is highly developed, and because of that, he can see, hear, and feel tiny changes in people and horses. He can see, hear, and feel things others can't, and that's because he's practiced being more aware. In my horsemanship, being aware can help me make wise choices with my horse and improve my timing, my feel, and my ability to recognize my horse's try. I need to develop my awareness to the point where I can see what my horse is *thinking* before he actually acts on that thought.

⋙◆⋘

In England, opportunities to work on my focus abounded. First off, of course, were the clinics themselves. As Mark's assistant, my job was to watch Mark work and then help the students who wanted to continue their work. I decided to give each session my undivided attention. I would focus on that session like there would be a quiz afterwards. I'd look for the small things in Mark's work, for patterns, and for new ideas in things I'd seen before. I would listen to what Mark said and to what the student said. I would listen to *how* Mark said what he said and *how* the students said what they said. I would consciously pay attention while I was on the job. I had always paid attention in the past, of course, but I wanted to see if I could get just a little better at it.

In Bristol, England, Mark did a two-day clinic, and each day there were about 200 spectators present. With that many people, little time went by without someone asking a question about what was being done in the arena. Mark always welcomes questions and seems to enjoy thinking about his answers. One afternoon in the middle of a rider's session, an audience member asked a question, and Mark asked me to take over teaching the student in the arena while he talked to the spectators.

Because I had been consciously focusing on the lesson and had a good feel for where Mark was going with it, I was able to step in and teach the student without a hitch while Mark answered the audience member's question. When he was done, Mark seamlessly stepped back in and picked up where I had left off. If I hadn't been practicing my focus at that time, I would have been a bit lost when asked to step in with no warning.

I also decided to work hard on remembering people's names quickly, practicing them in my head each time I saw them and using their name out loud at every opportunity. I ended up fielding a few questions from spectators myself and practiced my focus by listening fully to what people had to say, not interrupting them, and looking them in the eye with my complete attention for the time they were with me. When Mark and I set up and took down the P.A., I tried to focus on each wire and component as I handled it, so that when I was done, I would remember touching each piece and know where I put it. Interestingly, I found all this focusing to be exhausting, which goes to show how unfocused I was accustomed to being.

Inside the arena, I noticed the students struggling with their own focus. It's funny how when we begin paying attention to something (or "focus" on it), we start to see it all around us.

⸻◆⸻

In Scotland, I worked with a gentleman who was riding a four-year-old cob gelding that hadn't been under saddle very long. Understandably, the man was worried about his horse's greenness. Although the gelding was sweet and generally quiet, the clinic was a new experience for them both.

For this man and his cob, Mark and I concentrated on simple things like smooth transitions and getting cues agreed upon between the rider and the horse. Just as at most of our venues, I did my work with the students at the far end of the arena. Now, the far end of the arena was an exciting place in Scotland. The door to the outside was down there, and a lot of jump standards and other paraphernalia were stored there.

On the second day, I was working with the man and his horse on walk-to-trot-to-walk transitions, and everything was going well. We'd been at it for about fifteen minutes, when suddenly the cob spooked violently and spun. The man rode the spook admirably, and I suggested that he turn the horse around and just go back to what we'd been doing.

What the horse had seen were some folded-over black rubber mats that were in amongst the jump standards. What was strange was that he went past them for fifteen minutes before he spooked at them.

"Shouldn't I show those mats to him?" asked the rider.

"No," I said, "he's been past them dozens of times already today, and he knows they're there. We'll talk about it more in a minute."

We continued our work, and the horse spooked a couple more times, though much less violently than the first time. Just as the horse settled down again, the man burst out, "I can't stop thinking about those mats!"

Now, this was very interesting, because I had noticed the man looking at the mats since our session started. The horse had noticed, too. The man's focus was so drawn to the mats that he eventually drew his horse's attention to them. With both of them focused on the mats, there wasn't anyone focusing on the work at hand, and the horse spooked.

We discussed this, and we decided that no one would look at the mats anymore, and I included myself in that. None of us would move our focus to the mats and off our work. We worked for another forty minutes or so and the cob never spooked again.

Outside the arena, I also had many opportunities to work on my focus. I didn't always succeed, but I made a conscious effort. While we traveled in England, we traveled as quite a large party: myself and Mark, our clinic hosts Vanessa and Philip, Dr. Dave Siemens, Mark's longtime friend and equine chiropractor, and his wife Nancy. As it turned out, I was the only person in the group who'd brought an alarm clock, so it became my job to get up early and knock on everyone's doors to wake them for the day, since English hotels rarely provide alarm clocks in their rooms.

That may not sound like a big deal, but add jet lag, long days, late nights and early mornings, and getting up in the morning becomes an exercise in focus. When my alarm rang in the morning, I would imme-

diately think of my responsibilities for the day, not of how warm and cozy it was under the covers. That alone was an act of conscious focus.

At meals, I focused on using my knife and fork as the English do, fork in my left hand, knife in my right. I worked to focus on the conversations going on among us, and I tried to learn our waitperson's name and remember it for the evening. Little things, for sure, but then horsemanship is made up of lots of little things.

Awareness is something that I've learned a lot about since signing on with Mark. Mostly I've learned that I need to get much better at it. Mark can smell alfalfa on a horse, and he can see a horse relax his tail minutely as he travels. That's stuff that just passes me by, though I am getting better. It's always helpful to me when Mark points out what he's seeing or feeling, which he'll often do for my benefit during a clinic. Even while he's teaching someone else, he can teach me too. That also is awareness.

My work in England on awareness didn't go quite as well as my work on focus did. I found it very difficult to be always looking for things I couldn't see. I never seemed to know what the next layer of awareness I should be striving for was, so I felt like I was shooting at a moving target.

At the clinic in Devon, England, we met a woman with a nice black gelding that was pretty nervous about just about everything around him. On the second day of the clinic, the owner had removed her lead rope from her halter after bridling the horse, and I helpfully (I thought) walked over to take the rope from her so I could set it out of the way. My approach spooked the gelding, which hightailed it to the other end of the arena.

All I could think was, *What did I do?* Well, what I'd done was failed dismally where awareness was concerned. If I'd been watching that horse, as I should have been, I'd have seen he was not okay with me approaching him like that. But I'd only been looking at the woman and her lead rope. I'd have been better off if I'd taken in the whole picture in front of me.

Mark and the owner decided to take that opportunity to work on catching with the black gelding, since he was already loose. Mark started working with the horse, and the owner told him that the gelding did indeed have a catching issue, especially with strangers. Within an hour or so, Mark was able to catch and halter the gelding at will, and the horse obviously felt better about things. Mark recommended that the owner and I work on having me catch the horse later in the afternoon.

When the time came, we turned the gelding loose in a small warm-up arena off to the side of the main arena. He ran around quite a bit, as he had with Mark earlier that morning, so I did what Mark had done and broke up his patterns and just went where he went. It wasn't long before the gelding was turning in to walk or trot toward me, which I thought was a great step forward. But after he turned in toward me, he would walk or trot on by. If I stepped in front of him, he'd get scared and leave. I felt like I was missing something, but I couldn't figure out what.

I was able to get the gelding to let me pet and stroke him, but never got to haltering. I hadn't done much ground work with clinic participants' horses at that time, so I figured I'd done the best I could with him.

At the end of the day, when Mark and I were packing up the P.A., I asked him why the horse had walked or trotted past me after he'd turned toward me.

"You missed him offering to pass you right after he turned in," Mark said.

"But I didn't see him do that," I replied.

"He did it with me, too; it was tiny, but I saw it and shifted my weight left and right every time he did it, so when he asked the question, he got an answer."

There it was again, awareness. The movement the horse had offered had been so small that I'd missed it completely. As he had turned toward me (the offer to be caught), he'd wavered side-to-side a bit, offering to go past me. If I'd seen the tiny offer to go past, I'd have been able to direct the horse better so he could find a way to be caught. As it was, when his subtle offer went unnoticed, he went right past me. I just hadn't seen what I needed to see. For me, that was a lesson in improving my awareness wherever I could.

Interestingly, my awareness outside of the arena was nothing to write home about either. On our first day in Okehampton, we had checked into our inn and had the afternoon to ourselves. Mark, Dr. Dave, his wife Nancy, and I decided we'd go for a walk around town, looking at the shops and searching for lunch.

We exited the front door of the inn and turned right along the sidewalk (they call them "pavements" in the U.K.), heading toward the heart of town. I walked in the lead, and was the first to come to a street crossing about 100 yards from the door of the inn. I stepped into the road, only to have Mark grab my arm and pull me back onto the sidewalk as a car whizzed by only inches from where I'd been moments earlier.

Like many Americans, I'd almost fallen prey to the fact that the English insist upon driving on the left side of the road. For pedestrians, that means the closest oncoming traffic approaches from the right, not the left, as in the States. Lacking awareness can get you run over, I learned.

I'd heard Mark say it many times, "How we practice is how we'll go." I was practicing not being aware of my surroundings, so when I was with the horses, that's what I was good at. I was so unaware, I walked out in front of a car! I could see very clearly that the time for me to practice my awareness was in my everyday life.

I redoubled my efforts. I found that our inn was filled with tiny step-ups and step-downs—just big enough to trip on. I set out to never miss a step and to be aware, always, of what was in front of me. I tried to move through rooms of people without bumping into anyone. I counted how many people were in the restaurant or pub with us, and then added and subtracted when people came and went.

I tried to identify and separate the smells in a restaurant or pub—bread, beer, beef, chicken, wine, tea, sweets. I noticed the temperature of a room as I moved through it and was surprised to find that almost every room was not the same temperature throughout. When I tried, there were a myriad of ways to practice my awareness. I knew that if I practiced hard, I'd see that practice benefit my horse work.

When we returned from our trip to the U.K., I had a whole lot to think about. For perhaps the first time since I'd begun studying with Mark, I'd made a concerted effort to practice my horsemanship twenty-four hours a day. I found that if I practiced things *outside* the arena, it was easier to bring them *to* the arena.

So I began to practice my horsemanship as a way to be instead of practicing techniques. Mark talks about becoming a "student of the horse," and I think this may be part of what he's talking about. If we're a student of technique, which I have been in the past, we'll only get so far with things. But if we can become a student of the horse, the possibilities are infinite.

If we've focused on technique when we're with our horses, we may also tend to focus on our tools. A tool may be a special halter or lead rope, a whip or a stick, a rope, or any number of other objects. But the truth is, the best tool we have is with us all the time, wherever we go. It's *us*.

Now that's an interesting idea, because if the best tool I have to work with my horse is *me*, I've got *me* with me all the time, and I can practice my horsemanship all the time, wherever I go.

I got to thinking about that wholeness that I used to find with the horses when I was a kid. When I looked at that again with the idea of practice in mind, I could see that maybe what I needed to do all along was develop that wholeness within myself so I could *take it to* the horses instead of *taking it from* the horses. I figure I'll be chewing on that for a long time.

THE  BOX

A box has four sides, a bottom, and a top. A box does a pretty good job of containing things that are placed within it. The box I'm talking about here, in relation to horsemanship, is figurative. Being in a box in our horsemanship is kind of like starting to mop a floor at the doorway and mopping ourselves into a corner with no good way to get back out the door. Well, there's always a way out of a corner, but sometimes the solution isn't quite what we expect.

About six weeks after I had my stroke in 1994, I was walking down a sidewalk in Denver. Despite the fact that physical therapists had been repeating to me over and over every day for weeks on end—"Step up and step down with your good leg"—I stepped off a curb onto my weak left leg.

My left ankle turned under, and I did a pretty good job of spraining it. It felt horrible and was wonderfully blue and swollen for ten days or so, but since I was already seeing a physical therapist for my stroke rehab, I didn't see a doctor about it. The physical therapist iced it and treated it with ultrasound, and I continued with my recovery.

In April of 2000, I invited Mark to do a clinic in Aspen, where I was living at the time. We did a four-day clinic, in which I rode two horses each day, Ashcroft and a client's quarter horse. On the last day of the clinic, I was taking some jumps with Ashcroft when he stumbled going around a turn. My ankle gave a resounding *POP* as the force of the stumble turned it over in my stirrup.

I didn't know that a part of my body could make that kind of noise or be so darn painful. I wasn't sure if I'd broken it or if the ligaments had simply given way. I iced it, took a lot of Advil, and later rode my client's horse in her session. I saw an orthopedist the next day.

The news wasn't good. I'd torn just about every ligament in the ankle.

I entered physical therapy yet again to strengthen the ankle. I saw a man who made custom orthotics, and he constructed two special ankle braces for me, one for riding and one for hiking. I began hiking to strengthen my legs in hopes that brute strength could stabilize my left leg while I was in the saddle. But no matter what I did, my left leg moved and bounced as my horse moved.

Over the next few years, I sprained that left ankle an average of once a year, until in 2003, it became clear that something had to be done. I had an operation to tighten the ligaments in the ankle and rehabbed it yet again. Less than a year after the first surgery, I blew out all the ligaments a final time. In 2004 I had a second operation to graft new ligaments into the ankle. Shortly after I began working full-time for Mark in 2004, I had another surgery to install a metal plate in the ankle.

Now, the whole reason I was willing to go to the lengths I did to fix that ankle was because I wanted to ride as well as I could. The stroke had left me with some weakness in my left arm and leg, and once the ligaments in the ankle started to stretch out, it was difficult to tighten them up again. Each surgery made the ankle more stable, but each surgery also left me sore and swollen for six to nine months. By the time the spring of 2005 rolled around, I had been riding with post-op pain for over two years. The pain was like static on a radio that I had just learned to tune out as I went about my business.

———❖———

April of 2005 found Mark and me back on the road, headed for San Diego. We'd be doing two five-day clinics at Rancho Doblado, one of Mark's favorite places to work. In between the two clinics, we'd have two days off, and I was looking forward to riding Ashcroft on those days.

On our second day off, I saddled up Ashcroft and headed for the arena. Mark's horse, Mouse, had had his teeth floated earlier in the day, so Mark hung out to watch me ride. I trotted and cantered and had a little fun opening the throttle a bit, and not long into our ride, Mark came into the arena and stopped me.

"The movement in your lower left leg looks to be coming from your knee, not your ankle," he said.

Now, that was news to me, as I'd been living with that leg for ten years and Mark had been watching me ride with it for eight. How could the movement in my ankle be coming from the knee?

Mark popped over to the truck and got out a neoprene knee brace and suggested I give it a try. I put the brace on, snugging it up as tight as I could get it, got back on, and picked up a rising trot.

The change was instantaneous. My left leg bounced much less and felt more firm and secure around Ashcroft's barrel. It felt more like my right leg, for the first time in ten years.

"What else do you feel?" Mark asked.

I told him that I had a substantial pain in my lower leg, from just below the knee to just above the ankle, especially if I tried to turn my toe out. The pain was bad enough that I tended to position myself on the horse to protect against it. Thinking about it, I realized that in the last few years, my riding had begun to center around protecting the left ankle, and because of that, I was beginning to ride with some pretty significant bracing.

While I sat in the saddle, Mark put his hands on my lower left leg, and with his fingers, found the tendon that hurt when I tried to turn my toe out. Then he pushed hard on the tendon with his thumb, just below its insertion, about two inches beneath my knee. Then he had me lower my heel and turn my toe out a bit.

What should have caused a shaft of white-hot pain down my lower leg miraculously caused me no pain at all ... as long as Mark kept his thumb on the offending tendon.

"Bet you've got some tendonitis in there," Mark offered.

"How come?" I asked.

"That's just like what I've got in my arm, tendonitis right below my elbow. They gave me a band to put around my arm to put pressure on the inflamed tendon, and it works; it doesn't hurt. We should try it on your leg."

So Mark lent me the device, a Velcro band with a small pad made of gel. I positioned the gel pad over the tendon that hurt and tightened the band as tight as I could get it. Then I got back on and rode again.

I experienced yet another huge change. The pain in my lower leg was gone, and I could feel only a tiny bit of pain in the ankle itself. I was able to keep my left foot level in the stirrup and turn my toe out for the first time in ten years. With Ashcroft standing still, I was actually able to place myself in the jumping position, lifting my seat out of the saddle and supporting myself on my stirrups. I hadn't done that in years either; it had just been too painful.

I wore this new setup, knee brace and band, for the remainder of our time at Rancho Doblado. I rode in it and walked in it. Stabilizing my knee and addressing my pain level also improved my ability to walk normally and handle uneven terrain. I felt like I put my left foot on the ground flatter and more firmly. I was excited.

Now, what's interesting about this is that it shows what a "box" I was in. Ever since I'd had the stroke and sprained my ankle the first time, all anyone could see was that ankle. We rehabbed the ankle; we did surgery on the ankle; I wore braces on the ankle. Everyone was so busy looking at the ankle that we couldn't see anything above it, like my knee or my hip.

Because the doctors, I, and even Mark were thinking about the ankle so much, we couldn't see any other solution to the problem. Not until we "got out of the box" we were in could we see the thing differently and get some positive change going.

Climbing into a box is something that we do in our horsemanship as well. We sometimes get so we can't see the forest for the trees because we've talked ourselves into seeing something just one way. I've found myself stuck in a myriad of boxes in my horsemanship, and I spend a good deal of time these days trying to see the box before I get stuck in it.

⟫⟪

Back in the summer of 2004, I was spending about a week a month helping Mark out at his clinics in Loveland. In July I watched Mark working with Joe and his Arab-cross mare in the round pen. I was passing by, and I heard Mark say, "So Joe, what are you asking of her right now?"

I stopped and listened in, knowing I'd learn something.

"Well," Joe answered, "I'm asking her to pay attention to me. I don't want to ride her until she's paying attention."

"How's she supposed to know that's what you're looking for?" Mark asked.

I looked at Joe and his mare, and she was trotting around the pen with her head turned to the outside, while Joe stood stationary in the center of the pen. That meant that during half of each trip Joe's horse made around the pen, his back was to her.

"This is how I was taught to do this," was Joe's answer to Mark's question.

"Okay, but how's she supposed to know what you're looking for her to change?" Mark asked again. "You and I have been talking here for a couple minutes, and you haven't asked her to do anything different than what she's doing."

Joe looked a little stumped, and Mark asked if he could go in the pen with the mare and show Joe what he was talking about. The first thing Mark did was to move *with* Joe's mare. As the mare walked around the outside of the pen, Mark walked around the inside of the pen with a similar amount of energy. Then Mark sped up his walk, and the mare began to trot.

"Now she and I are doing this work together," Mark said to Joe. He continued to do some upward and downward transitions by walking faster or slower, sometimes backing up that cue by raising a hand or kissing.

Joe had been taught to work with his horse a certain way, but with this particular horse, it wasn't working so well. When Mark showed Joe another way to do the same work, a way that got Joe and his horse interacting, the horse was happy to pay attention. It looked like Joe's horse probably thought that when they went in the round pen, she was *supposed* to tune out, because Joe hadn't asked her to do otherwise.

Joe worked the mare in the round pen himself again, and a nice change came over both of them. Joe was happier with what his horse was offering, and his horse seemed happier with the fact that she was getting a little more direction.

I think Joe had mopped himself into a corner with his mare. At one point, someone he respected told him that this was the way to work with a horse in a round pen. And on that day, with whatever horse it was, that may have been appropriate. But on that day in Loveland, Joe wasn't getting what he needed, and he wasn't doing anything to change what *he* was offering so his horse could change what she was offering. Joe needed to get out of the box he was in and see things a bit differently. He found there isn't only one "right" way to do things.

At the very same clinic, Mark asked me to work with another student who was riding her horse in the arena. I rode in, and Ashcroft and I stood just inside the gate, where we'd be out of the way of the people riding and able to observe the entire arena.

The student was riding at the trot, and things were going very well. We worked on softness and upward and downward transitions, and I had the student stop by my horse to chat a couple times. Then a funny thing began to happen. The student's horse began to speed up whenever he was heading toward the gate. So we worked on that for a while, but it didn't improve very much.

As the student and I struggled with this new issue, Mark quietly rode up on the other side of the arena fence and simply said, "Kathleen, why don't you move your horse over there somewhere and see what happens?"

I didn't know why he'd suggest that, but I did move my horse to the other end of the arena. Immediately the student's horse stopped speeding up as he headed for the gate. It hit me like a ton of bricks that it wasn't the *gate* that horse was being drawn to, it was *my horse*! The simplest way to fix the problem was to just move my horse, instead of doing a lot of training with the student's horse. For the rest of the session, I moved my horse from place to place in the arena, and the student's horse stopped quickening his pace without being asked.

I had assumed the student's horse was being drawn toward the gate because I was in the box that is my old teachings—"Horses are lazy and deceitful." And then, even if I'd gotten out of *that* box, I'd have been in yet another box, governed by the idea that moving my horse would have been "cheating." In that one situation, I trapped myself in multiple boxes, when really, if I'd been focused simply and exclusively on helping this student and her horse do what they needed to do, the boxes would have fallen away, and Mark wouldn't have had to point out what should have been an easy answer.

━━━━━◈◆◈━━━━━

We can also get in boxes related to our disciplines or our breeds. We can get in a hunter/jumper box (my usual box), we can get in a gaited-horse box, and we can even get in a "natural horsemanship" box. At Mark's clinics, we tend to see a lot of people who are in a "natural" box.

There really isn't a single thing we do with our horses that is natural for them. The moment we put a halter on a horse, selectively breed him for generations, and fence him in, natural is out the window. And who says natural is synonymous with good? The tsunami in Indonesia was natural, but it wasn't a good thing for hundreds of thousands of people. Arsenic, black widow spiders, and radiation are perfectly natural, but they're not good either. So for me, just because something is "natural," I don't assume it's good.

But a lot of times, we want to do things with our horses "naturally," because that somehow means we're doing things better than those people who aren't "natural." I'm not even sure all this "natural" stuff is about the horses; I think it might be about people wanting to label their work and set themselves apart from others. In the end, "natural" or not, our work will speak for itself. I don't think that horses really care whether something is natural as long as it helps them in their lives.

While we were in England, we got the impression that the English are very interested in "all things natural" for their horses these days. We saw a lot of barefoot horses, and Mark was asked many questions about it. Most of the barefoot horses we saw were very happy that way, but one was not.

The horse was a bay thoroughbred mare that had previously been an eventer. Her owner, a very knowledgeable and kind older woman, said that when she'd gotten the horse, her feet had been very poorly shod and were cracked and horribly out of balance. The owner had done a lot of research into alternative care for horses' feet and decided that the mare would be better off barefoot. She decided on a type of barefoot trim that would be best for the horse and found a barefoot trimmer that specialized in that trim.

When we saw the mare, the owner told us she'd brought her to the clinic because she had trouble catching her and had trouble with impulsion under saddle. Mark had her walk the mare around, and it didn't take long to see where some of her problems were coming from. The horse had been barefoot for over eighteen months, but she was still awfully footsore and appeared to be very uncomfortable. In my eyes, the mare moved like a horse that had foundered badly.

Mark talked with the owner about the horse's history and about her desire for the horse to be barefoot. The woman told Mark her trimmer had said that the horse could be sore for quite a while after going barefoot and that he didn't think this horse was that sore. Taking this into consideration, Mark asked the owner to see Dr. Dave Siemens, the equine chiropractor with us on our trip, to see if he could clear up some of the horse's obvious stiffness and pain.

Mark took a look at the horse the next day, and she didn't look much better. Dr. Dave had found a lot of things on the horse that needed work and had done that work. Now that the horse's joints were looser, it was even more obvious to me that her feet were hurting her.

Mark had another talk with the owner, this time suggesting that perhaps the time had come to try putting shoes back on this horse to relieve some of her pain. Perhaps if she was shod *well*, her feet could be healthy and she could be comfortable. Eighteen months, Mark said, was a long time for a horse to be lame.

"Just consider it," he asked of her, as he also promised to give her money back for the clinic, since she hadn't been able to ride.

That mare had been in pain for eighteen months, and when you only live thirty years or so, that's a big chunk of your life. The owner, in her admirable desire to do what was best for her horse, had committed to a certain course. But she'd also gotten a bit stuck in the "barefoot box" and couldn't see another way out.

"If the only tool we have is a hammer," I've often heard Mark say, "everything looks like a nail." It was time to get that horse some relief, one way or another, inside the box or out.

Around about May, Mark begins his summer clinics in nearby Loveland. Mark and his wife Wendy begin planning the clinic schedule for the next year at the same time. Scheduling clinics is a complicated business, when you look at putting together the invitations to give clinics with time of the year, proximity to other clinics on the same trip, driving distances, holidays, family birthdays, and important school events.

For weeks, when I'd leave the Rashids' house in the morning, Mark and Wendy would be bent over the computer working on the schedule, and when I'd come home, they'd still be there. Each year, Mark gets dozens and dozens of clinic requests, and in addition to that, he's got a bunch of places he likes to go to every year. Then there is the East Coast, where he tries to go every two or three years. And every time he goes to England, people beg him to go to Europe. But there are only so many days in the year and only so many places he can get to.

Each year, the schedule reflects a hard-won balance between work and family, between new places and old places, near places and far places. Each year, Mark is out of town for a couple important things—a birthday here, a gig with the band there, an anniversary, or some other special day. Mark's family is pretty pragmatic about it, maybe because they've been doing it for so many years that it's normal now.

As I go through my horse work these days, I struggle with my own "hunter/jumper box." I spent over twenty years in the hunter/jumper culture, and it is, for the most part, what I know. In fact, I still participate in the culture. I learned it well enough that I was able to teach it, and teach it I did. Therefore, every so often, something I've been doing forever crops up and begs to be examined.

About five years after I began riding with Mark, Ashcroft began to stop at jumps here and there. One of the things I'd always liked about Ashcroft was that he would jump anything, from anywhere, any time. But as I began to improve my horsemanship, he began to let me know when I was doing things that made his job more difficult than it should be. One of the ways he did this was by stopping at the jumps. If I was making that job just *too* hard for him, instead of sucking it up and doing it anyway, he'd just stop and let me think about it a bit.

As soon as spring came, I began to spend some extra time preparing my horses for our upcoming summer horse show season. On our days off, I'd scrounge out some jumps if I could and work Ashcroft a bit. I planned to start showing as soon as we came home to Estes Park for the summer.

The weekend after our first week-long clinic in the summer of 2005, I entered a Colorado Hunter/Jumper Association-sponsored horse show not far from Loveland. The first day of the show went very well, and Ashcroft and I won a second, a third, and a fourth in pretty stiff competition. Ashcroft felt good, and I thought I was doing a really good job of using the show not to "show off" per se, but as an opportunity to practice my horsemanship, to do what I do.

The second day of the show, we had a stop at a black-and-white oxer, just three jumps into our first course. As is usual when I get a stop, my first reaction was to try again right away, which I did. Another stop. We tried again, and he went, but we had yet another stop later in the course, which dismissed us from the class. This would need some thinking about.

I took Ashcroft to a quiet corner of the warm-up ring, where other riders were preparing their horses for the class. I thought about what I was doing that was different than the day before. I thought about what Ashcroft felt like as he stopped, how far he was from the fence when he stopped, and what he felt like the day before. If I'd had to sum up what felt different between the two days, I'd have said I felt more "joy" in him the first day of the show.

So I sat and I thought, and as I did so, snatches of what the trainers in the warm-up ring were saying to their students floated in and out of my consciousness. Then it clicked; the solution came to me from one of the trainers in the ring. "Put your leg on. Squeeze!" she shouted at her student.

How many times had I heard Mark tell students about how a horse moves, how he has to be able to move his barrel out of the way of the back foot that is going to step up underneath it? In Oregon, hadn't I *myself* advised a student whose horse was stopping at the jumps to take her leg *off* her horse so it could move and jump? Hadn't that horse only stopped faster, the more leg she'd put on it, and jumped happily when she took her leg off?

I had been at that horse show (in the hunter/jumper box *big time*) for a whole day, watching people squeeze their horses with their legs to get them to jump. For a whole day, I'd heard trainer after trainer say, "Leg, leg, leg, spur!" And it had seeped into my own work, by osmosis, unbidden. I *knew* my horse knew his job and didn't need me nagging him every step. I *knew* that the more leg I put on him, the greater were my chances of getting a stop. I *knew* that the tighter my legs were, the less his barrel could move, and the less his legs could move. But it sneaked up on me all the same; I had let what others were doing influence me, and I'd climbed right back into that box while I wasn't looking.

I figured we certainly couldn't do any worse than elimination, and I decided I'd keep my leg *off* Ashcroft in our next class. I squeezed him once to pick up our canter, and then I made a concerted effort to just leave him to his job. I thought about the two of us doing this job *together*, not about me telling him what to do and wondering what would happen if he didn't.

The change in our work was instantaneous and real. He jumped fluidly and joyfully, happily accepting my guidance, as long as I didn't make his job more difficult by instructing him. I kept my leg off, and he actually went faster on the whole than he had before. He certainly moved more easily and jumped better. It felt like the joy was back, for both of us.

I got to thinking about that experience later in the day, as I packed up my stuff and loaded my horses to go home. Even though I had been on this path I'm on with my horsemanship for about nine years, it was so easy to be influenced into climbing right back into the box I'd worked so hard to get out of. I discovered that I could be tempted back into the box without realizing it.

⟫◆⟪

I believe that horses don't profit when we get stuck in our thinking. Horses live in a world of feel, not technique, a world of sounds and smells and sights. They adapt and blend and change with the world around them. They haven't read the books that tell us people what we can and can't do with them, and I think that to them, something is "correct" only if it helps them. They're not worried about where the helpful thing came from or how pretty it looks or who thought it up.

Mark once told a story about a woman who bought a pony for her kids from some people who were passing through her town. Now, this is my version of the story as I remember it, but I think the point will remain the same even if the telling is different. The pony was broke to death and kind and gentle with her kids. The kids grew up riding that pony all over the local countryside, doing things with it that unsupervised kids tend to do with ponies.

A few years after the woman bought the pony, she ran into the person who sold her the pony, and she told him how fabulous that pony had been for her kids and about some of the adventures they'd had with it.

He listened to the story and then told the woman, "You know, that pony's blind as a bat."

All that time, those kids had ridden that pony as though she were fine, and she was fine. Not knowing she was blind had enabled them to avoid putting that pony in a "blind pony" box. All that pony knew was that those kids never steered her wrong. And all the kids knew was that the pony had never steered *them* wrong.

When we put ourselves or our horses into a box, we limit ourselves to that little box—top, sides, and bottom. If we stay in that box, we may never have the chance to discover what else is out there or what is possible outside of those familiar walls. If our goal is to be *with* our horses, I think we're more likely to find them outside a box than inside one.

CONFIDENCE 5

"The only difference between me and you," Mark said to the student as I passed by, "is that I'm not afraid to make mistakes and you are."

Ouch. I felt like I'd been caught out as I walked by the round pen where Mark and his student were working, like some cosmic force had made sure I'd overheard the only part of Mark's comments that I needed to hear.

It made me think pretty hard about how we horsemen, myself not least among us, get caught up in all kinds of fears: fear of failure, fear of upsetting our horses, fear of upsetting our trainers, physical fear of our horses, fear of getting hurt, fear of doing the wrong thing. Gosh, I could go on and on. And all those fears, if we let them, can paralyze us to the point where all we can do is sit and look at that horse in the pasture and admire his coat, because we can't bring ourselves to do much else.

Confidence in ourselves is something we don't often think of as an ingredient of good or successful horsemanship. But the more I watch and listen and learn at Mark's clinics, the more I start thinking that maybe confidence is one of those little-appreciated things that can truly make or break our horsemanship. It may be one of the few things that separates great horsemen like Mark from good horsemen like myself.

We horsemen spend a lot of time perfecting our techniques, working on our feel and timing, and finding the right equipment, but we don't do a lot of work on our confidence or other qualities of character. Technique and feel and timing and equipment are all necessary, but what we take to our horsemanship in addition to all that stuff is *who we are*, warts and all. Behind everything are our attitudes and beliefs and history. Here's where that niggling thought can come in, more powerful than any technique or piece of equipment: *This won't work. I'll never get this. I'm not a horse trainer.*

A technique delivered with the thought *This won't work* behind it may very well *not* work. But the same technique delivered with the belief *This will work; one way or another, it'll be fine* behind it most likely will. That may sound kind of trite, but I have found it to be true, especially with horses.

Any piece of knowledge or any technique has something behind it—*attitude*. In large part, our attitudes are made up of the things we say to ourselves and the things we believe. If we believe we're a crummy horse trainer, we probably will be. If we think we're a good horse trainer, we probably will be.

———⟫•◆•⟪———

Starting in late May, Mark begins his series of clinics in Loveland, less than an hour's drive from his home in Estes Park. This enables him to work every other week and be home every evening while the kids are out of school for summer vacation.

A maximum of seven horses and riders are accepted at these week-long clinics. Everyone rides all day, working on their own things, while Mark and I circulate around offering help and advice as needed. Every morning begins with a meeting and some unmounted exercises. The exercises help give the students a feel for and an understanding of some of the more theoretical ideas we work on with the horses, such as "softness," "blending," and "the power of thoughts."

We can talk until we're blue in the face about how helpful it is to "blend" with a horse's unexpected movement. But until a student has actually *experienced* what blending feels like on the ground, it's pretty hard for him to do it while his horse is spooking, for instance. If we provide a feel for the concepts, we hope that it will become easier for the riders to link them to their horses.

The day after I overheard Mark's comment about fearlessly making mistakes, we did an exercise with the students in which they pair up with one person becoming the "horse" and the other the trainer. The "horses" don blindfolds, and then Mark secretly gives each trainer a task to teach his or her partner. The trainers stand behind the "horses" with a hand on each shoulder, and they may not talk to them or touch them anywhere else.

At that clinic, we had a woman named Mary, who was a fairly green horseman, and she'd brought her fairly green four-year-old horse that she'd started herself. She wanted to see how she'd done with him so far and to learn to communicate better with her young horse.

Mary paired up for the blindfold exercise, and I watched her work with her "horse." Mary's task was to encourage her partner to climb up a stack of hay bales, pick up a stick on top of the stack, climb down, take the stick to the opposite end of the barn, tap a specific chair with it, then go back up the hay stack, and put the stick back. Considering that her partner was blindfolded, it was no mean feat!

Mary calmly guided her partner through all the tasks, and they were one of the first pairs to finish the exercise. When everyone was done and we were discussing how things had gone, Mary's partner was surprised to see with her own eyes what she'd done under Mary's guidance. She also said that Mary's direction had been clear and concise, even though she couldn't see what she was doing. She said she'd been comforted by Mary's soft but assured guidance.

Now, this was fascinating to me. Here Mary was, teaching someone to do something they had no concept of. There were no agreed-upon cues for them to use; they'd just made it up as they went along. But Mary had believed she could lead her partner to do those things without troubling her. That confidence was clear to her partner. That confidence was key to their success in the task.

What Mary did that day is very similar to what we all do every time we work with our horses. The horses are like the blindfolded people in the exercise, in that they can't really "see" where we're going with the things we work on with them. What's kind of miraculous is that they're okay with that, for the most part.

The horse just wants to do things with the least amount of trouble possible. When we enter the picture, with all our self-doubt and second-guessing, that just makes his life a bit more bothersome than it needs to be. And as long as we have self-doubt or second-guess ourselves, our work with horses is more about us than it is about the horses, and I'm not sure that's fair to them.

—⟫•⟪—

Not long after that experience, I spent a weekend spectating at a large hunter/jumper show in Estes Park. I especially watched the jumpers, who work against the clock.

Among jumpers, there's a kind of culture-wide fear of the "Liverpool," a blue plastic pool with water in it that competitors are required to jump over. Some riders are so concerned about it that they buy a Liverpool and put it in their horses' stalls or paddocks for them to live with.

At the horse show that weekend, I watched a parade of riders deal with the Liverpool. Some riders rode in and just put their horses to work, jumping the prescribed course. Other riders rode in and made a beeline for the Liverpool, where they "showed" it to their horses. A few of them even took their horses over to it and then spanked them with their crops.

Over the course of the afternoon, a trend appeared. Riders who didn't show their horses the Liverpool, by and large, had no problems with it. Riders who did show it to their horses, in general, had some sort of trouble with it.

This got me to wondering why some horses had problems with it and others didn't. Sure, training comes into it, I suppose, but jumping horses are jumping horses because they generally like to jump and are good at it to some degree. In the course of their jobs, they see a myriad of different kinds of obstacles, but the Liverpool just seems to be the most problematic of them all.

As I watched, I began thinking about confidence again. The riders who didn't show their horses the Liverpool obviously didn't because they assumed or already knew that it wasn't going to be a problem for them. So they had confidence.

The riders who showed their horses the Liverpool, on the other hand, appeared to lack confidence. After all, they thought it necessary to go over and show the jump to their horses ahead of time, so they must have been operating on the assumption that it was going to cause problems for them. Sure enough, in many cases, that assumption was borne out.

By the end of the afternoon, I was pretty certain that it was the *riders*, not the horses, who had trouble with the Liverpool. Let's look at their practice of showing the jump to their horse upon entering the arena.

Having lived in that culture for over twenty years, I know what they were intending to do. They meant to say to their horse, "Hey horse, just so you know, there's a Liverpool over here, so don't be surprised when we come around that corner and here it is." I'm guessing that the riders who spanked their horses by the Liverpool were intending to say something like, "Don't even think of not jumping this Liverpool!"

Let's look at this situation from the horse's point of view. He's a jumper. He knows how to jump; he's been doing it since he was a baby. He's been doing it with a rider at horse shows for at least a couple years and maybe a lifetime. He enters the show arena full of jumps, and he's got a pretty good idea of what's expected of him—he's supposed to jump what's put in front of him.

Then the rider takes him over to one particular jump and points it out to him. So now this jump is special somehow. He doesn't know why; he just knows now that his rider is concerned about this particular jump. Maybe what he hears the rider saying is, "Just so you know, horse, I'm really concerned about this Liverpool, so when we come around this corner I may just lose my mind." And the horse that gets spanked, maybe he hears, "Bad horse, for coming over here by the Liverpool!" So here's the horse, not unlike Mary's blindfolded partner, just trying to do a task for the trainer. But the trainer has already decided there's a problem.

What's more useful to our horse? What's more helpful to him? We can look at our work and assume it will turn out okay one way or another, or we can assume we're going to make a mess of it. Either way, I bet we'll be right.

In July, Mark and I flew again to England, where we would do three clinics and then fly back home to continue the summer clinics. By now, I was loving going to England and was excited to see the countryside in the summertime. In winter, the grass and hedges are still green, but in summer, all the trees would also have their foliage.

As usual, we flew Economy Plus for the extra legroom and planned to sleep as much as we could on the way over. As we boarded the plane and got ourselves settled, Mark and I noticed that the first class cabin was utterly empty. Mark told me that when he'd taken his family to Scotland for a vacation a few years ago, they'd been offered first class seats since they were available. I began to get a little hopeful. I'd never flown first class anywhere, let alone England.

Sure enough, before long, a British steward stopped by. I looked at him expectantly. He looked at our felt cowboy hats, which Mark and I were holding in our laps. Traveling with hats is a bit of a trick, since they're expensive and you don't want them to get crushed. We never put them in overhead bins to avoid them ending up under someone's carry-on case. On this flight, we were seated in the first row of the section, so there weren't even seats in front of us to store them under. So they sat in our laps.

The steward, glancing up to the empty first class cabin asked, "Could I please take your hats for you and store them in first class for the flight?"

Mark and I exchanged a glance, and I had a hard time keeping a straight face as I handed the steward my hat. On that flight, our hats went first class, while we gazed at them from Economy Plus.

England was as green as I thought it would be. The countryside was lush with grass and trees and flowers and creeping vines. It was lovely and hot, as well, which was a nice change from the cold of the previous January.

On one of our days off, our hostess Vanessa took us up to see the moors in Devon. Moors are basically big open spaces. The moors in Devon are grassy, with hills and rocks and bogs. Wild ponies live up there, mostly privately-owned herds of Shetlands that are rounded up once a year for maintenance. Vanessa told us that due to the fact the only contact the ponies have with people is fairly traumatic for them, they're uncatchable and not very friendly.

We drove through the moors, up on top of high hills, past gorse bushes and over bogs. We reached a band of ponies, and Vanessa stopped the Land Rover so we could get out and watch them. I checked out the ponies, which just kind of looked like regular ponies to me, then enjoyed the general scenery. When I looked back to our group, Mark was gone. I glanced toward the band of ponies, and there he was, steadily making his way to a small, youngish-looking bay pinto. I was fascinated.

It took Mark about fifteen minutes to get up to pet the pony. It never ran off and it never got very concerned. Mostly it looked what I would call "politely interested" as Mark worked slowly with it, in and around several other ponies. When he did get up to it, he stroked it once on the head and left the band.

Back in the Land Rover, I asked Mark why he'd decided to go pet the pony. It had been an unexpected opportunity, he said, to practice a few things he'd been working on in his horsemanship. It was an opportunity to practice his craft. He hadn't thought such a chance would come again soon.

"Why that pony," I asked him, "when there were several others that were closer and older?"

"That pony said it would be okay for me to do that; the others didn't," he replied.

"How did it say that?" I asked.

"In a lot of ways—you could just see with that pony, it was going to be all right."

Well, I figured I'd take his word for it, because I still didn't quite understand, and I had a feeling he'd given me a bit less than the whole answer.

Horsemen aren't much different from anyone else working to hone and master a craft. Except for some reason, we seem to expect to get it "right" more than we get it "wrong."

I think we'd all agree that Babe Ruth mastered the game of baseball. Even those of us who don't necessarily have a passion for the game know who he was. Babe Ruth had the confidence to step up to the plate and point to where he was going to put the ball. And then he did it.

If you look at Ruth's statistics, he had 8,399 at bats. He hit 714 home runs. He struck out 1,330 times. That means he went to bat and did NOT hit a home run 7,685 times. Heck, he had more strike-outs than home runs. But he was considered a master of his craft.

Each time Ruth walked up to the plate, it was possible that he'd strike out. It was also possible that he'd hit a home run. The possibility of striking out didn't keep him from going to the plate. If he didn't go to the plate he wouldn't strike out, but he also couldn't hit a home run.

Willie Shoemaker is a legend in American thoroughbred horse racing as one of the sport's winningest jockeys. Shoemaker rode in 40,350 races in his career. He won 8,833 of those races. That means he "lost" 31,517 races. Yet he kept going to the post, day after day. He'd never have amassed over 8,000 wins if he hadn't gone to the post so many times. I think it'd be safe to say that Shoemaker didn't expect to win every one of his 40,350 races. The prospect of coming in somewhere other than in front didn't keep him home.

⧦◈⧦

How often does fear keep us home? When we work with our horses, how often does our fear become a self-fulfilling prophecy? How often do we not try something just in case it doesn't work? How often do we set up excuses for ourselves or our horses before we ever get started?

When I began working for Mark in 2004, it was a big deal to me. I'd been working hard on my horsemanship for years, and here was an opportunity, an opportunity I'd probably never have again, to live and breathe horses, with someone for whom I have the utmost respect.

But looking at it that way was pretty scary. What if I made mistakes? What if I didn't measure up? What if, worst of all, I disappointed Mark?

The first couple of months I worked for Mark, I was riddled with fear and self-doubt. I've never been physically scared of horses, but I have been and continue to be scared of making mistakes, which can be just as paralyzing as being physically frightened.

"The only difference between me and you is that I'm not afraid to make mistakes and you are."

I've had to think a lot about that. When you get right down to it, if we're not willing to make mistakes, we don't have a lot to work with. If I approach a horse and I'm not willing to mess up, then I'm probably not going to offer him anything very valuable. He may be the one horse who needs me to try something I've never tried before. He may need me to make it up and be willing to just work and work until it's right.

I didn't make a lot of mistakes as a kid. I did what I was told, got good grades, and came home on schedule, every time. I didn't like the feeling of making a mistake, even back then, and I still don't. But what I'm starting to see is that mistakes are inevitable, and furthermore, that if we're not making mistakes, maybe we're not working hard enough to go where we haven't gone before. I want to improve my horsemanship, I want to master it, and I want to do that without making mistakes. Fat chance.

———◆———

When we were in Texas in September of 2004, I'd gone out to do Mark a favor and catch his horse, Mouse. I'd met Mouse once just after Mark had picked him up the previous year, and I knew that Mouse was pretty troubled about some things. I approached him carefully, not wanting to scare him.

When I got up to him, he presented his right side to me, so I went with that and moved to halter him from the right side, which scared him silly. He ran off, and as I regrouped, I thought something like, *Great. Now he'll never let me get near him again.* But I figured I better try again, only this time from the left side.

So I headed for Mouse again, this time making it clear to him by my approach that I intended to handle him from the left side. To my surprise, he let me walk right up, halter him, and lead him off.

When I think about that now, I realize that with Mouse, I made an honest mistake. I didn't know he was really touchy about being handled on his right side. Call me crazy, but I think Mouse recognized that my mistake was an honest one, forgave me immediately, and let me try again with no hard feelings. My mistake enabled me to learn something, and if I hadn't made the mistake, I would not have learned those things. And as for the horse, he was okay with me making the mistake as long as I tried my best not to do it again.

To horses—and to people, for that matter—there's a difference between making an honest mistake and making a careless or malicious mistake. It's about what's behind it. If I am doing my best, if I am trying hard, then maybe I can make mistakes confidently. And if I can make mistakes confidently, perhaps someday I'll be a really good horseman.

———◆———

Not long ago, while Mark and I were in California, we picked up my new horse, Maggie. She's a seven-year-old buckskin grade mare that had come to a clinic and that I'd fallen in love with and wheedled away from her owner. Maggie had been this woman's reserve horse, the horse she rode when she couldn't ride her others for one reason or another. She'd been trail ridden and could walk, trot, and canter, but she was really still pretty green.

We brought Maggie home and then went back out on the road to do some more clinics, so I left her back in Estes. When we returned, I rode Maggie two or three times and then loaded her up to take her to a horse show to participate in a couple of flat classes.

As far as I knew at the time, Maggie had never been to a horse show. She'd been to a couple clinics with her previous owner, and having only ridden her a few times, I didn't know her very well. But I made the decision that I was going to use Maggie's first horse show as a way to practice my confidence. I took Maggie to the horse show with the attitude that everything would be fine because I would show her the way and not get her in over her head.

As I saddled her up for her first class, she felt very confused to me, like she had no idea what we were doing there, which was understandable. I rode her in that class with about twenty other horses and showed her at the walk, trot, and canter. Although she felt confused, she did what I asked.

She had a bit of a rest, and then we went back for another class, again in a ring packed full of other horses. This time she felt completely different, as if she'd thought about it and now knew what she was doing. I kept her out of harm's way and guided her through the class, and all went well.

When I got home from the horse show and chatted with Mark about how good she'd been in the big groups of horses, he reminded me that one of the things her previous owner had wanted to address was the trouble they had in groups of horses.

I had simply forgotten that the mare was uncomfortable in groups, so I took her to that horse show expecting her to be fine. And she was. It was the Liverpool all over again. If I'd thought Maggie was going to have trouble, she may very well have. But as it was, I assumed she'd be fine and that I could show her the ropes, and that's what happened.

Like many other horsemen out there, I'm not as good a horseman as I want to be. My knowledge and experience can use improving, of course. But the fact that I don't have all the pieces to the puzzle yet doesn't mean that I can't work with the puzzle pieces I *do* have with confidence.

SOFNESS

When I first sought Mark's help with Ashcroft, I was, in all honesty, looking for a quick fix. I wanted some things I could do to make that horse get his act together. I certainly was *not* looking for a way for me to be.

At that first clinic with Mark, I heard him say things like, "That's a nice look there," "There's a change," and "There, that's softer." It was all Greek to me. I couldn't see anything he was talking about. All I knew was whether the horse was or wasn't doing what I asked him to do. And sometimes Mark said the horse was doing good things even when he wasn't doing the appointed task. I didn't get it.

How could the horse be doing something good, even though it wasn't what we asked for? There was simply nothing in my life experience or my experience with horses that equipped me to answer that question.

⟫◆⟪

Horses are born into a world quite different from our own. Only days after birth and with no help from us, they can do lead changes, cross water, piaffe, spin, and do sliding stops. They can sort grain from dirt with their noses. They can turn and stand on three legs to scratch their ear with a hind foot. As a herd, they can move as one, like a field of wheat undulating in the wind.

All that wonderful stuff is already there, available to horses and to us, if we can just avoid taking it away from horses as we work with them.

There's a common denominator in all those things that horses can do, and that's softness. When Mark said Ashcroft was doing something good, even though he wasn't yet doing what I asked, I think Mark saw softness. Mark knew something I didn't back then—softness can be the key to the mint, so to speak.

Horses are born with softness, and so are we. Both horses and people lose it along the way, I think, and then find it's a struggle to get it back. It would be easier all around if we didn't lose it in the first place.

⟫◆⟪

So what is *softness*? There are a lot of layers to it. In order to define it, we have to start somewhere, and my definition is going to start in the middle. My intention is not to be cryptic, but because softness is a way to *be* and a *feel* rather than something we or our horse do, we might have to get a bit cryptic before we can be less so.

At its simplest (and perhaps most cryptic), softness is that place where everything is available. When our horse is soft, he can physically go anywhere from where we are: from a stop to a walk, a trot, or a canter; from a canter to a stop, walk, or trot; from left to right; from powerful to languid; from scared to nonchalant; from worried to relaxed. If there's softness there, the transition is effortless because from where the horse is, everything is available.

If we are soft, we can be the same way. Wherever the horse goes, the horseman can go, too. If the horse canters, the rider goes with him. If the horse spooks left, the rider can move left with him. If we're soft, everything is available: tiny bits of pressure, lots of pressure, quickness, slowness, waiting, forging ahead, going at things sideways or backwards, or going at things straight on.

In order to find softness in our horse, we have to give it, and that means giving everything we have to the horse, with no strings attached. I don't claim to know how to do that yet, but if I could, that would be softness.

This layer of softness is what enables us to have those mystical moments with our horses, where it feels like we're just borrowing his feet. We think it, and he does it—in that movement is all the power, all the quietness, all the quickness, all the slowness, all those disparate qualities, all at once. They're right there, and we can feel them as they float up from the horse and through us. That's softness.

Another layer of softness is encompassed in the idea of "as little as possible, as much as necessary." This is a nice general rule and may at first sound trite. But if we think about it, this is again about how we *are*, not necessarily what we do.

When we work with a horse, if we can offer a small thing first, the horse has a choice to respond or not. If he responds, we've successfully gotten a change with a small cue. If he doesn't respond, then our adage dictates that we be willing to find a way to get a change, using "as much as necessary."

At Mark's clinics, we see the full gamut of people struggling with this idea. On one hand, we see people who grew up similar to the way I did. They tend to look for what the horse is doing wrong and almost itch to make a correction. They tend to use more than is necessary to get something done and then correct the horse when he objects. This amounts to a lack of softness, as the rider and the horse fight back and forth, mentally and/or physically.

On the other hand, we see people who aren't willing to do "as much as necessary" to encourage a change. Sometimes they just don't know how, and other times, they're more concerned that their horse "like" them than that they help the horse learn. This also constitutes a lack of softness, in that not all possibilities are available if we're not willing to do what's needed at the time.

Being as soft as we *want* to be is sometimes different than being as soft as we *can* be. If I have a situation with a horse where I'm in physical danger of being run over, say, then I am not able to be as soft as I *want* to be. But the important thing is that I should be as soft as I *can* be with that horse, in that situation.

Being "soft" doesn't mean I or my horse turn into a doormat. This is a common misconception. That's not soft, that's weak. Softness requires that we retain our point of view through the process. Soft isn't necessarily slow, soft isn't necessarily easy, soft doesn't necessarily look a certain way for every horse, soft isn't necessarily the path of least resistance. But soft is, well, soft.

<hr />

Softness also has a purely physical layer to it. Softness exists when we and our horses are using the fewest muscles possible to accomplish a task. The opposite of soft is a brace, where we're using more muscles than are necessary. Horses, being programmed for physical economy, tend to be soft when they're out on their own, because being braced is highly inefficient.

Softness is key to achieving the maneuvers we're looking for with our horses, from going down a trail to the piaffe and passage, from the spin and sliding stop to a big, round, explosive jump. Softness provides movement and possibility. Bracing limits movement and possibility.

A good example of bracing that we see fairly often at the clinics is the horse that travels inverted, meaning that his head is high, his back is arched downward, and his hindquarter is trailing behind him. This is a very inefficient way to travel since the horse has to tense all the muscles in his topline, thus restricting the movement of both his spine and his legs. If he traveled that way out in the wild, he wouldn't last long.

A horse that travels softly, however, has switched off the muscles of his topline and engaged his abdominal muscles to support himself, which enables his back and his legs to move freely. A horse traveling softly will have the suggestion of an upward arch from poll to tail. His nose is down, his withers up, and his hindquarter engaged. He is traveling very efficiently, especially for carrying a rider.

A person or horse is soft when he's using as many muscles as necessary to get the job done and no more. So we end up back at "as little as possible and as much as necessary."

⟫·◆·⟪

When Mark talks about softness, he makes a distinction between "soft" and "light," which I think is important. According to Mark, "soft" occurs on the inside of a horse, while "light" occurs on the outside of a horse. Another way to look at it is that softness is responsive, while lightness is reactive. We can have lightness without softness, and we can sure mistake lightness *for* softness.

If a horse is light, he might be very responsive to the aids, he might be kind of jumpy, and he might exhibit behaviors without being asked. He might look well-trained. A horse that is light might also do things by rote, without thinking or engaging his insides. He might perform but be tuned out mentally. That's lightness, not softness.

A horse that is soft will sense a request, *involve* himself in the request, and then offer a response, although he may offer something other than what we want. A horse that is soft will perform the maneuver or skill with his whole self—his body, mind, and spirit. He won't be thinking one thing but doing another. He will back up wholly; he won't back up physically but be thinking "forward." A horse that is soft will look and feel entire, congruent, and harmonious.

For people, it's the same way. We ourselves can be light without being soft. We can say things that sound soft, while thinking something completely different (and decidedly *not* soft). We're being light if we become a doormat in our desire to be soft. Being soft requires that we retain our point of view, that we acknowledge what's true and right and not give that up. If we can practice that in life, then maybe we can take some level of it to our horse work.

<hr>

Mark has been practicing the martial art of aikido for many years and uses what he learns to help him work more effectively with horses. When I began working for Mark, he offered me a membership to the dojo (the martial arts school) so I could practice if I wanted to.

In June, after Mark and I had started the summer-long series of clinics, I finally made the commitment to begin studying aikido. I had been going to the dojo and watching classes and talking with Mark about aikido for a few months. It took me that long to decide to get started, mostly because I was scared.

One of the reasons that I decided to start aikido was because I trusted that it could teach me much about softness. From my discussions with Mark, I had learned that aikido is a purely defensive martial art. You couldn't use it to start a fight, for instance, because the moves just wouldn't work. The aikidoist actually uses the attacker's energy to diffuse the situation.

Furthermore, for aikido to work, the aikidoist has to be soft—not dead-fish soft, but "what's-right-and-true" soft. The aikidoist must have good intentions and a genuine desire to help his attacker out of the spot he's gotten himself into. A good aikidoist, it seemed to me, must be a master of softness. Softness is what I saw in Mark's horse work, and I wanted to get better at it myself.

Starting aikido was one of the hardest things I've ever done. I felt out of place, out of my comfort zone, awkward and clumsy. But I wanted to learn, to practice aikido, to experience being a beginner again, and to improve my horsemanship. From my very first class, what I got were lessons in softness.

When I went to each class, I tried really hard to leave my self-consciousness at the door. I figured I couldn't learn if I was afraid of looking stupid. I knew that I wouldn't be able to take in the information or feel the moves with my body or smile to my teachers in appreciation. What I felt when I wasn't afraid was softness—a softness in me that allowed the learning to take place.

As a beginner in aikido, I have very little skill yet. I don't know what softness will *feel* like in the techniques. But I can see how important mental softness is to the process of learning, and that's what aikido has taught me so far. To be open to learning requires softness, and since I hadn't been a beginner in anything for so long, I think I'd lost sight of that kind of softness.

The softness I needed had to come from inside of me, and it wasn't easy. The softness I needed was about accepting correction and advice without feeling bad about myself. It was about going to class for an hour-and-a-half and trying as hard as I could the entire time, not just when it was convenient for me. It was about doing the best I could, even if that wasn't very good, and being happy with that. Not satisfied, but happy. And even more, that softness was about being open and humble and actively and honestly looking for ways to be better.

⪻◆⪼

We're all students of one thing or another. If we're horsemen, we're students of the horse. As time went along, I had forgotten about the "beginner's mind," about the softness of being a student. After we do something for a while, we begin to think we've got a handle on it, and we lose that softness. But if I can keep the softness of a beginner's mind, I can perhaps adapt, learn, and grow—in life and in horsemanship—on a more consistent basis.

When the summer clinics were finished for the season, we had about a week off, and then in early October, we packed up and left for eastern Washington and Oregon for a series of clinics. Every trip I'd been on with Mark had gone very smoothly, but that two-day trip to Washington gave me the opportunity to think about softness in yet another way.

At the very beginning, our trip began to twist and turn. As we loaded the truck first thing in the morning, we found it had a flat tire, and our departure was delayed as Mark took the rig to the local garage to get it fixed. When he returned, he didn't rush or even comment on our delayed departure. We just finished packing, loaded the horses, and got on our way.

We traveled through southern Wyoming and then north toward Jackson Hole and the Tetons, where Mark planned to head west over Teton Pass to Victor, Idaho, where we would spend the night at a friend's place, as we had on our last trip up that way. But when we headed north out of Rock Springs, we picked up a strong head wind, and the clouds began to turn black on the horizon. By the time we reached Jackson, it was snowing and blowing, and a call to Mark's friend in Victor told us that our plans would be changing. Teton Pass was closed to trailers until morning, and any detour to Victor would take almost two hours.

Mark stopped and thought for a bit. He decided that we'd go over to the fairgrounds to see if we could hole up there for the night. When we got there, we found all the facilities locked except for the parking lot. We pulled the horses out there, fed and watered them, and let them have a rest, though we didn't want to leave them out in the cold, wet, and wind for too long. We got out the maps and Mark's computer with trip-planning software and looked at our options.

We were due in Washington for a demo the next afternoon, so we need to get close enough that we could get some rest during the night and still arrive in Washington on time. Since we couldn't go over Teton Pass, the most direct route to the Northwest, we either had to backtrack south or go north through Yellowstone National Park. Mark decided we'd go north and shoot for Bozeman, Montana as a stopping place for the night.

We pulled out of the fairgrounds around 8 P.M., with the horses relatively rested. The road through Grand Teton National Park was in good shape, but as we neared Yellowstone, the conditions steadily worsened. We met a park ranger who kindly advised us of the only open route through Yellowstone that night and wished us luck. It took us five hours to get through Yellowstone, with much of that time spent creeping at five miles per hour down hills covered in ice.

At about 2 A.M., we pulled into Livingston, Montana, just short of our goal of Bozeman, and found a truck stop where we could get a few hours' rest while the horses rested, ate, and drank again. We hit the road around 7 A.M. and uneventfully made it to Washington for the scheduled pre-clinic demonstration.

That whole trip was a study in softness. At no point did I see Mark brace against what was going on. Sometimes he had to stop and think, but he never once complained or wished he was somewhere other than on an icy mountain road in the middle of the night. He worked with what came up and just got on with things. He handled that trip the same way he handles horses.

If we look at the layers of softness that I talked about earlier, we can see all those elements in that trip. First, everything was available to Mark: going fast or slow, waiting or forging ahead, changing plans or keeping them the same, taking advice or making his own decisions. Most profoundly for me, he'd even asked me to see if there was a route we could take to the east, opposite from the direction we needed to go. I hadn't even thought of it. But to Mark, every option was available.

On that trip, Mark also used as little as possible but as much as was necessary, over and over. We went as far as we had to that night and no farther. We went as fast as was safe and no faster. We were as easy on ourselves and the horses as we could be, but we got done what was necessary. He expended as little energy as he could but as much as he had to.

Mark was physically soft as well. While I found my neck and shoulders getting tight as we crept down those icy roads in Yellowstone, Mark's hands were relaxed on the wheel, and we chatted about how ironic it was that my first trip to Yellowstone was in the dark. Sure, he was tired, but he accepted that softly and found a place to stop and rest.

⧫

In Washington, Mark was scheduled to give two three-day clinics and a five-day clinic before moving on to northern Oregon for a four-day clinic. Given the circumstances of our trip out, I found the idea of softness in the forefront of my mind as we did our work in Washington.

One of the horses had trouble backing up. Scout could back up in the pasture by himself just fine. Mark checked him out for physical issues and found him to be sound. He checked that Scout's saddle fit comfortably, which it did. His bridle fit, and he was happy with his bit. But when his rider, Mary, asked Scout to back up, he would sidepass to the right instead. At some point in the past, Mary may have inadvertently led Scout to believe that the cue to back actually meant "sidepass right" by releasing the "back up" cue when Scout sidepassed right. Mary wanted to clear up this misunderstanding, so Scout could back up *and* sidepass to the right with different cues.

As Mark worked with Mary and Scout, it became clear that they were both bracing in many ways. Scout was bracing physically by tensing his entire body and refusing to go any direction but right. He was also bracing mentally in that he was unable to consider that the cue he was receiving might mean anything but "sidepass right." Scout wasn't being stubborn or disrespectful or "bad;" he was simply offering a behavior he'd inadvertently been taught was correct.

When Scout sidepassed, Mary braced against that movement because it wasn't what she wanted. The harder Mary pulled on Scout, the more he braced against her. If Scout sidepassed all the way over into a fence and ran out of room, he reared up rather than backing because he couldn't think of anything else to do. It turned into a vicious cycle for Mary and Scout, with one brace leading to and feeding another.

Before he could back up, Mark said, Scout would need to soften up his mind and consider that the cue he was feeling might mean something other than what he thought.

"A horse," Mark said, "will offer what he *does* know before he offers something he doesn't know."

Scout would offer everything he could think of before he would come upon the "new" idea of backing, and Mary would need to stick with him and give Scout feedback as he searched for the response she wanted.

Mark helped Mary present the same information to Scout over and over, which was basically, "This means back up, this means back up, this means back up ..." While she was doing that, Scout offered the sidepass, pawing and stomping, throwing his head, and rearing. In amongst all this movement, Scout eventually accidentally offered a step backward, and right then, Mark had Mary release her cue.

Scout was pretty shocked by this and stood there for a moment blinking. I think at that point, he didn't really know what he'd done to get the release. Mark had Mary ask him to back again, and Scout struggled almost as much as the first time, but within all his movements came a step back, and he got an immediate release.

Mary repeated this process over and over, and Scout found that step or two backwards a little faster each time. Mark told Mary that Scout had to try all the other things he was doing before he could find those steps back. Mary stuck with him, and within fifteen or twenty minutes, Scout was finding those first steps back very quickly.

Mary's session with Mark ended with Scout able to back up softly, with his head down, jaw relaxed, poll flexed, neck relaxed, and hindquarters engaged. Mary was also much softer, as she now understood how she and Scout had become confused and how to clear up the misunderstanding. Mark had helped Mary establish a cue that became mutually understood between Mary and Scout, so she could use it softly and Scout could respond to it softly.

———⋙◆⋘———

At the same clinic, we worked with a woman who had difficulty leading her horse. When Tracy entered the round pen with her horse, he bumped into her repeatedly and circled around her. Mark asked if that was normal behavior. Tracy acknowledged that it was and said that the horse often reared while being led as well.

Mark asked Tracy what she did when her horse reared up. She told him that the people where she boarded the horse, who did "natural horsemanship," had told her that if the horse was rearing, she was putting too much pressure on it. Based on that advice, she had been backing off when he reared. Tracy said that she was trying to find a "soft" way to show the horse that rearing was not a desired behavior. She said she really wanted to get along with this horse and wanted him to like her and like being with her.

Mark asked how long the horse had been rearing and if the behavior had been getting better or worse. Tracy said the horse had been rearing for six months or so, and it had gotten slowly but steadily worse.

Mark asked to work with her horse, and he started by teaching Tracy's horse a few simple ground rules, the first being "Don't run me over," which Mark says is his only non-negotiable rule. It didn't take long for Tracy's horse to offer the rearing behavior that had earned him so many releases from pressure in the past.

Unlike Tracy, Mark did not step away when Tracy's horse reared. Instead he redirected that horse's energy by encouraging him to go backwards. Sometimes, Mark said, horses rear because they can't back up, and sometimes they run people over because all they can think of is to go forward. Being able to back out of a situation gives them another option.

I know that Mark did a lot of other things that I couldn't see, but the end result was that in a very short time, Tracy's horse had all four feet on the ground and was leading nicely for Mark, then for me, and then for Tracy.

The situation Tracy had gotten into with her horse is actually common. Tracy's case is pretty extreme, in that her horse had developed a dangerous behavior. Where Tracy had gotten off track was in her desire to be so "natural" and "soft" that she ended up not getting the job done. When her horse began to have trouble, she wasn't able to see that in order to be truly soft she might have to first go somewhere that wasn't as soft or pretty as she wanted it to be.

What Tracy did, in a nutshell, was give up her point of view. She needed to be safe, but she gave that idea up for fear that her horse wouldn't like her. She also wasn't willing to do as much as necessary to get the job done, so she lacked softness in that way as well. Tracy's intentions were good, of course, in that she wanted her horse to be happy, but she just got lost in her attempt to be "soft" in ways that weren't truly soft.

What happened with Tracy and her horse can happen to anyone, including me. I want my horse to like me, I want to have a nice time with my horse, and sometimes I just plain don't have the time to deal with things that come up. But in the end, I've got to make a decision about how important softness is to me, in my horsemanship and in my life. If I want to master softness, I have to try to live softly, whether it's convenient or not.

<hr />

I've been hearing Mark talk about softness at his clinics for many, many years. He talked to me about softness at my very first clinic with Ashcroft. I loved the idea then and began to make it a priority in my horsemanship. It was an elusive idea and an elusive feeling. The one thing I *did* figure out about softness was that once I had something to where it was soft, it could always be softer still. There was always another layer of softness underneath.

While we were doing a clinic one summer, Mark offered me the chance to ride Mouse. I'd met Mouse not long after Mark purchased him nearly two years before, and he was a bit of a mess, to be frank. He had been a roping and ranch horse for most of his seventeen years, and at the time I met him, he kind of hummed like those high-tension power lines that you just don't stand underneath because it doesn't feel safe. Over time, Mouse had come right on around, and when Mark offered to let me ride him, Mouse and Mark were doing some very beautiful work together.

I knew from watching Mark with Mouse and from hearing him talk about his work with Mouse, that Mark cued him primarily by *thinking about* or *picturing* what he wanted Mouse to do. So when I climbed aboard Mouse that day, I knew that I was probably going to feel a layer of softness that I wasn't very familiar with.

I started with some easy stuff such as just walking forward, which I cued for by picturing Mouse's feet in a four-beat walk and by thinking about walking forward myself. I cued for turns by picturing Mouse's inside front foot leading the turn. We did a couple of stops and walk-to-trot transitions.

Everything Mouse did was soft in a way I hadn't felt before. It felt as though, with every step, he was checking in with me and saying, "What do you want? Where are we going now?" I found myself "coasting" a few times, and I missed some of Mouse's questions.

As I got ready to give Mouse back to Mark, I did one last stop with the intention of returning to the walk. From the stop, I thought about the four-beat rhythm of the walk, and underneath me, I felt a peculiar sensation. Mouse himself didn't move in a physical way, but inside, he made a complete circle.

What on earth was that? I thought to myself. I paused and then thought about the walk again, and I felt Mouse make another mental circle underneath me. Finally it dawned on me—what Mouse was doing was offering every direction, every point of the compass, and waiting for me to pick one. When he came around to "north" or forward, I said to myself, *That's it*, and he walked off.

With Mouse that day, everything was available and everything was offered. I can't think of anything softer than that. That ten-minute ride taught me volumes about softness and gave me an inkling of where I could head with my own horsemanship. I had no idea that that kind of softness could exist between a horse and a person. I'd been striving for softness for years, sure, but I had no idea that it could feel like *that*.

Suddenly, something I'd heard Mark say in England made a lot more sense. It was one of those times when I just overheard a phrase as I worked with a student at the other end of the arena. I'd heard him say, "When I ride my horse, I want to give everything I have." I'd pondered long over that, slowly chewing on it and digesting it, over and over.

After riding Mouse, those words meant more to me. In order for Mouse to offer everything to his rider, his rider must first offer everything. It has to be a fair exchange.

As I contemplated this, it occurred to me that in my own life I hadn't yet offered everything I had to anything: to any job, person, aspiration, goal, or horse. That, I decided, needed to change.

MEAN 7 WELL

Meaning well or the lack of meaning well is one of those things that underlies and colors our horsemanship. When we work with our horse, do we mean to help him, or do we mean to "make" him? I think there's a big difference to the horse.

The first time Mark ever said anything to me about meaning well was back when I was still a student, at a clinic to which I'd brought a client's horse for some extra help.

"When you go in there," Mark said to me, as I put my hand on the round pen gate, "you need to mean well."

When I heard that, to be honest, my first thought was about how doctors take the Hippocratic oath and that somewhere in that oath is the pledge to "first do no harm." Did Mark mean something like that?

Little did I know that of all the things I would contemplate and work on in my year as his assistant, this idea of meaning well would haunt me the most. It would come up over and over, with a myriad of variations. I would struggle with it, wrestle with it, and hate it for its obstinate presence in my life and my work. Even now, I don't claim to have a firm grasp of the idea. But I hope to, someday.

⟹⬥⬦⟸

If you watch closely at Mark's clinics, you'll notice that he enters the pen, arena, or workspace a certain way. If he's on horseback, he backs into the space if he can, and if he's on foot, he enters the space with his left foot first. This ritual has its roots in Mark's aikido training, he told me.

In the days of the Samurai warriors, they were in the habit of carrying swords. Most of them were right-handed and carried their swords on their left hip. It was easy to draw the sword if the right foot was forward and more dif-

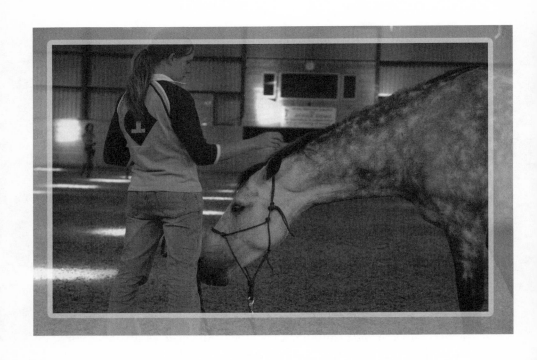

ficult if the left foot was forward. Therefore, if a Samurai entered a room with his left foot first, he was making it awkward to draw his sword and telegraphing to all present that he was entering in peace, meaning no harm, meaning well. Entering an area on his left foot is, Mark said, a way to remind himself that he is entering that space in peace and means no one inside any harm.

Martial artists study their art in dojos, where they can practice in a safe and supportive environment. Many martial artists enter the dojo on their left foot, as a nod to the Samurai and to remind themselves that they mean no harm as they go about their work.

Of course, we can mean no harm and still do harm. That has a lot to do with our skill level. As a lower belt in the dojo, I have very little knowledge of aikido, and the responsibility I bear to do no harm is limited by my skills. But a brown or a black belt has a lot more responsibility, because his or her knowledge—and the possibility of doing real harm—is so much greater. As one's knowledge grows, so does one's responsibility to do no harm.

This applies to horses, too. Mark tells a story about a call he went out on as an animal abuse investigator for the state of Colorado. He went to check on an undernourished horse. When Mark asked, the owner said that she'd been religiously feeding the horse four times a day. He asked what she was feeding it, and she said a loaf of bread four times a day, just like the person who sold her the horse had told her to.

She didn't know that a "loaf" is part of a bale of hay or that four loaves of bread was not enough food for a horse. With some education, she changed what she was doing and the horse did well. Because her knowledge was limited, she wasn't held to be as responsible as a person with greater knowledge of how to feed horses. This woman meant well, but she didn't have sufficient knowledge to feed her horse properly.

Although there are no brown belts or black belts in horsemanship, the more we know about horses and the more we try to accomplish with them, the more responsibility we have to do no harm. It's not simply a matter of meaning well, but it certainly starts there.

⟫◆⟪

The way I grew up with horses, meaning well wasn't a "core value" espoused by the system I was a part of. We gave it some lip service, but I don't think we were serious about it. Most of what I learned was based on the belief that horses are lazy and dim-witted, and I can't think that exemplifies "meaning well." But that's what I learned, and when it came time, that's what I taught.

I can remember taking ponies I was training and tipping them over onto fences, where I'd hold them up with my foot against a board until I was ready to right them again. I sure didn't mean well when I did something like that. Looking back on it, I'm not even sure what I thought I would accomplish with such a stunt. Maybe it was just a way for me to vent my frustration at not being able to figure things out when I got to the bottom of my toolbox. I was just so caught up in my frustration that I couldn't see the horse's point of view. I know for a fact that's what happened with Ashcroft in the beginning.

———— ◆ ————

Meaning well, I think, is also about taking the focus off ourselves. This is really hard, as it appears that we all practice considering ourselves first, and as you know, we get good at what we practice.

When I began working with Mark full-time, I felt self-conscious twenty-four hours a day. I was super-aware of every awkward move I made, every tiny mistake, and every word I said in his hearing. All that took a lot of energy and most of my awareness and focus. I didn't have a lot left over for the job itself. I think now that it also made it hard for me to mean well, because my focus was so directed at myself.

I would be the first person to admit that I haven't completely gotten past that focus on self. It's a process and it goes at its own pace. Besides, it's a scary thing to take our focus off ourselves. After all, if we don't look out for ourselves, who will? Who will be our advocate, our moral support, our ally?

It can be really hard to see past ourselves to the things around us that are bigger than we are. We're not just "ourselves," we're one individual in a family—a graduate of a school, a representative of a circle of friends, a single member of a team, a small portion of numerous communities. Our fortune is tied to theirs simply because of our membership in them.

It's the same in our dealings with horses. Our fortune is tied to theirs, simply because our paths have crossed. Our work with them can easily become about us, instead of about the horse. What if we could give up our need to shine so that the horse could?

And it's not just about our horse work. What if we could do that in other things, too? What if we could fade away and the thing we were working on could take on a life of its own through our involvement with it? What would that be like? What if, in order to truly mean well, we need to fade into the background, so to speak, so that our work, and not we ourselves, becomes what lasts?

⋙⊶⊷⋘

I used to struggle a lot with things my horses did. I felt like they were doing things *to* me. I suppose, as a kid, I'd heard my instructors say, "Don't let him do that to you," one or two too many times. Maybe that isn't really what they meant, but that's what I learned. I ended up looking at the not-so-good things my horses did as things they did *to* me. And then the good things they did were things they did *for* me. That's not the way to mean well.

We see a lot of people at Mark's clinics who have this point of view, and I still do myself sometimes. But now that I have devoted more thought to it, I understand that my horse is just offering behavior, behavior that is *horse* behavior with little moral value. He can canter corners just as well on either lead; it's us who put the value on the horse leading with the inside leg. It's us who wants the flying change from the hindquarter first or wants the horse's head to be here or there or somewhere in between. I think it really doesn't matter to the horse much of the time.

But then he does something we don't want. Say he jumps and we part ways. A lot of times we hear this described as, "My horse threw me." Well, it's possible that the horse simply jumped for a reason of its own, and we fell off. The horse did a horse thing, and then we did a human thing. Sometimes, just in the way we talk, we're playing a bit of a blame game, and that doesn't help us mean well.

Meaning well entails being willing to believe the best about our horse, our friends, our job, our situation ... whatever. Our horse didn't do that *to* us, he just did it. It seems that there's always a bigger picture. If we get tunnel vision and only see our tiny part in it, we can't see how the pieces fit together.

⋙⊶⊷⋘

Back in the summer while we were teaching week-long clinics, Mark had a "word of the day" that he gave the students each day. That word was expounded upon during our unmounted exercises for the day and was mentioned in context by Mark and myself whenever the opportunity arose.

One of the words of the day was "help." For me, the most striking thing about the idea of help was that it is only help if the recipient sees it as such. We can all remember times when we've wanted to help someone do something, and we know darn well they had to go back after we were gone and redo whatever it was that we "helped" them with. That wasn't help, because the recipient of the help probably didn't see it that way.

It's the same with our horses. For instance, if my horse gets a little too forward, perhaps I'll shut him down and ask him to stop and back up to get him doing something different. Maybe he keeps getting forward, maybe even more forward than he was before I started "helping" him with this problem. If that happens, then my horse isn't seeing what I'm offering him as help, and I need to try something else that he *will* see as help. What I think should be helpful and what my horse thinks is helpful might be two different things.

When it comes to meaning well, I believe we can *think* we mean well, and it can even feel like we mean well, but if the recipient doesn't see it as such, then it isn't meaning well.

⇒•⇐

At a clinic in Hood River, Oregon, we met Maddie, a young horse that had been started at three and had shown prodigious talent. Because of that, she'd been pushed too quickly to do things she didn't fully understand, and it caused her to become reluctant to work. Becky, her owner, said that Maddie both bolted and balked and also found simple requests very difficult to execute.

At the beginning of her session, Maddie jumped around quite a bit between balks. Mark asked Becky what she'd been doing with Maddie, and she told him that because the horse had been pushed so hard at a young age, she tried to put very little pressure on her. She mostly limited her requests to things Maddie volunteered to do. That consisted of walking and trotting in the arena when Maddie offered it. Becky hadn't ridden her outside the arena because that hadn't seemed safe.

Mark encouraged Becky to offer Maddie more direction in what she was doing, and on that first day, he had her ask Maddie to do simple patterns of straight lines and ninety-degree turns. The idea, he said, was to provide Maddie with some guidance while giving her success at something simple so she could feel good about herself.

Each day, Becky directed Maddie more and more, and Maddie accepted her direction cheerfully for the most part. Becky and I continued the work Mark started each day, focusing on turns and straight lines, then simple walk-to-trot and trot-to-walk transitions. By the fourth day of the clinic, Becky was riding Maddie around the arena calmly and cheerfully with no balks or bolts.

Becky told me she had thought she was helping Maddie by being very passive and unobtrusive during their rides. If too much pressure had bothered Maddie, no pressure would be better. Now she realized that she'd actually left Maddie with little guidance or support. Becky had seen her passivity as helping Maddie, but Maddie hadn't seen it as help.

It may not even have been the pressure that bothered Maddie, but simply her seeming inability to do anything right. When Becky used a reasonable amount of pressure to ask Maddie to do something and then released it when Maddie offered the desired behavior, Maddie was successful and wasn't bothered by the pressure. When she understood that a particular cue was linked to a particular behavior, she didn't mind doing it.

From what I saw, Maddie and Becky weren't that far from what they each wanted. Maddie wanted to understand what to do and when, while Becky wanted Maddie to be rideable, calm, and happy. The only little glitch had been Becky's decision to back off and leave Maddie alone. Maddie wanted guidance, but guidance she could understand and respond to successfully.

———◆———

At the clinics, we see quite a few situations where the person thinks they're helping but the horse doesn't. I still find myself in that position, where I mean well and want to help my horse, but I don't really know what will help. What I'm finding is that providing guidance is a good way to offer help and to mean well.

When Mark and I picked up my new horse, Maggie, I didn't really know much about her. I knew she'd gone out on the trail some and that she could walk, trot, and canter in the arena. I also knew that she wasn't completely averse to the idea of jumping, as I'd taken a couple of small jumps with her in California.

With Maggie, I really wanted to concentrate on this idea of meaning well. Here was a new horse, with whom I had no history and with whom I could try some new ideas. I wanted to see what Maggie thought was meaning well and what wasn't.

A couple months after bringing Maggie home, I began to work on jumping. I started with poles on the ground and little jumps she could just trot over. From the beginning, her jumping was inconsistent. Sometimes she'd rap the poles with her feet or hit them hard enough to send them flying. Other times, she'd jump so high and so hard that it was a challenge to just stay in the middle. I thought about this quite a bit and worked on figuring out what I wanted to accomplish with Maggie and how.

With Maggie, I wasn't so concerned about the jumping part of it to start with, but her inconsistency seemed out of character, so it had to be coming from me somehow. I felt like I was being consistent in what I offered her. I was trying to mean well and help her by staying out of her way and letting her handle the jump.

Finally, I asked Mark to take a look at what we were doing. After watching ten jumps or so, each of which turned out differently, he said, "She's just looking for some guidance. She wants to know what to do. Because you're not telling her, she's kind of grasping at straws."

I'd made the same mistake Becky had. In wanting to help my horse, I'd left her to her own devices, which hadn't been helpful at all. I saw clearly that in order to mean well, I had to offer Maggie what she needed, not what I *thought* she needed. After a couple of tries, I should have realized what I was doing wasn't helping and tried something else. But I was so convinced that my way to help was the best way that I couldn't see past it.

I also found that I was riding Maggie the way Ashcroft liked to be ridden, and as it happened, she didn't like it. What was helpful to him was not helpful to her at all.

When I offered Maggie more guidance, she jumped much better and much more consistently. By way of guidance, what I did was suggest to her the amount of impulsion we would need to jump, where to take off, and how high to jump. With my experience, those were things I could help her with. I believe she perceived that guidance as help, as she improved dramatically as soon as I made the change.

As horsemen, it's our job to ride our horses like we'd like them to be,

but we also need to make adjustments for each individual horse. I would like Maggie to end up being confident and soft over fences. But I couldn't necessarily *start* there. I'd forgotten because it had been so long, but Ashcroft didn't start being confident and soft over fences either.

When we have to help our horse in a way that we don't want to, we need to remember that it's not forever; it's just for now. Tomorrow it could be different. In six months, it will no doubt be different. If we don't offer any help, it will never be different. I may not like needing to help Maggie so much with jumping right now, but it's not forever. What she sees as help will change as she learns and grows. Then it's my job to change with her.

⟹◆⟸

As sensitive and perceptive as horses are, I am confident that they can feel the difference in *us* between a desire to help them and a desire to make them do something. Meaning well entails putting our own agendas and baggage and boxes aside so that the horse can benefit, even perhaps at the cost of a benefit to ourselves.

When I watch Mark work with a horse, there's a certain feel and look to it. He's not worried about the clock or about what people might think of him and his work. He just wants that horse to feel better as soon as possible, that's all. When he pats a horse and says, "There you go, bay horse," *that* comes from his heart, and there's nothing more important to him in that moment than helping that horse get along better. That's meaning well.

On that trip from Colorado to Washington and Oregon and back, we put on over 3,200 miles and crossed five states twice. Our trip out took us through Yellowstone in that snowstorm and had been a bit circuitous, and our trip home took us back almost the same way so we could pick up a new horse in northeastern Wyoming. Mark had been in negotiations to buy a horse off a ranch there, so it made sense to go over on the way home and pick it up.

We left Hood River about 5:30 P.M., after finishing up the last lesson on the last day of the clinic, packing up, and saying our goodbyes. We hoped to make it almost 700 miles to Bozeman, Montana that night, where we could get the horses out and have a short sleep before pushing on another 200 miles to Lovell to pick up the new horse. Then it would be about 500 miles back to Estes Park. We planned to be home the evening of the day after the clinic ended.

We pulled into the ranch right on time, after driving through much of the night and catching a three-hour cat nap in Montana. At the ranch we met up with Steve, who showed us Mark's new horse, a big red dun gelding with a blaze and four white socks that we'd later name "Scooter." I unloaded Mouse and Maggie in the driveway, hung a hay bag for each of them, offered them water, and cleaned out the trailer, while Mark and Steve went away to do business.

I hung out with the horses, enjoying the big blue sky, the birds singing, and the balmy Wyoming sun on my face. When Mark and Steve reappeared, they had someone with them, a big man with a warm handshake and shy eyes. Steve introduced him as Jack Blankenship.

"Jack's a cowboy poet," Steve said as Jack blushed. "Recite something for them, Jack."

"Well," Jack said slowly, "I don't really do that anymore."

But with some encouragement, Jack did recite a poem for us there, in Wyoming, in the sunshine, surrounded by horses, 500 miles from home. As he told it, he'd been asked by some friends to write a toast for their son's wedding. Jack had declined, claiming that once he agreed, then he'd have to write something and that would take the fun out of it.

A day or two later, Jack and Steve went out on horseback to work cattle, and when they returned in the evening, the wedding blessing had been created. Jack said he'd gotten to thinking about a team of pretty used-up draft horses he'd seen at a sale and what that team had maybe been through together. The picture of that old team had formed the idea for his wedding blessing.

I got to thinking about Jack and his wonderful poem later as Mark and I headed south through Wyoming. Jack had been asked to do a friend a favor, and though he'd declined, it was as if he couldn't help but do something nice for a friend. It was almost as if he'd done it despite himself.

I think that was because whether Jack knew it or not, he meant well toward the person who'd asked him the favor, and that desire to mean well is what carried the poem forward—with Jack in tow.

It loses something without Jack's interpretation and his Wyoming drawl,
but I'd like to share it with you. It went like this:

> *It's called trav'lin' in double harness,*
> *or jumpin' over the broom.*
> *Tyin' up the weddin' knot,*
> *or hitchin' a bride and groom.*
>
> *Yessir, it's got lots of names,*
> *monikers by the slew.*
> *To label this here ceremony,*
> *that ends with "Yes, I Do."*
>
> *But these doin's are just the start,*
> *then all the work begins.*
> *So if I give any advice,*
> *it's "you best start out as friends."*
>
> *'Cause friends is folks you pick,*
> *for reasons that are sound.*
> *They may not be rich or pretty,*
> *but you like to have 'em around.*
>
> *Anyhow riches dwindle,*
> *and pretty fades away.*
> *But if your hearts are knit,*
> *they'll most likely never stray.*
>
> *I guess the best example,*
> *is an old work team at night.*
> *When turned into the corral,*
> *they never swap it left for right.*
>
> *They go everywhere in tandem,*
> *never leavin' one another.*
> *Keepin' a good eye peeled,*
> *to protect their life-long brother.*

Oh, they'll gladly take a kickin',
so's not to pain their pal.
Please pay attention, Pard,
that's how you best ought treat your gal.

And when hooked to the bob-sled
and the goin', it gets tough.
They tend to encourage one another,
it helps 'em through the rough.

You'll see 'em rubbin' on each other,
after their oats are ate.
I plead with you here girl,
show your man that you appreciate.

Now when the world gets heavy,
and oh, it surely will.
Won't you think of that old team,
I call 'em Bob and Bill.

But one thing we ain't covered,
is who has got the lines.
'Cause no one's on this earth
by their own designs.

So start each day on your knees,
and seek your Lord above.
Ask 'im to show you how to forgive,
and also how to love.

Never go to bed mad, or fail to
give your love a squeezin'.
See, when they made that harness
double, they made it for a reason.

BREATHING

8

One of the first times I focused on breathing while working with horses was two or three years ago, when I took Ashcroft to one of Mark's clinics and asked him to help us with a stopping problem we'd developed in our jumping.

One of the things I'd always loved about Ashcroft was that he didn't stop; he never had, from the very beginning. He would jump anything, from anywhere, and I could take him into the show ring knowing, at the very least, that we'd have no problem getting around the course without any stops.

That changed suddenly when Ashcroft began stopping at jumps in the show ring. At first, I thought he might have a soundness problem, but when I had him checked out by both a vet and a chiropractor, they agreed he was feeling pretty good. I made sure my saddle still fit and had his teeth examined. Everything checked out. I was baffled, to say the least.

Ashcroft's stops weren't violent or "nasty," as we'd say in the hunter-jumper business. Sometimes, four or five strides out from a jump, he'd simply do a nice transition to a stop, even putting his head up so I could use his neck for balance if I needed to. He wasn't upset or distracted or scared. He'd just stand there and wait for me to circle him off to try again. Sometimes he'd stop again and sometimes he'd go ahead and jump the second time around. I tried "spanking" him with a short jumping crop when he stopped, as that's what I'd been taught to do when horses stopped. It didn't help. He wasn't bothered by the spanking, and it didn't keep him from stopping again.

At the clinic, the stopping issue was tops on my list of things to work on. I told Mark what was going on and then set up some jumps so I could show him. Sure enough, within three or four jumps, Ashcroft stopped. And stopped again. Then he jumped a couple and stopped again. Mark had me keep trying while he watched and thought.

Finally he asked, "Are you breathing at all when you're jumping?"

"I couldn't tell you," I answered truthfully.

"Well, go do it again and see."

So I did, and as it turned out, I was catching my breath and holding it right after I turned the corner and got lined up straight to the jump. I could feel it, I told Mark. But I didn't know why it mattered.

"The thing is," Mark said, "because you're holding your breath over the jump, Ashcroft's having to land really hard, and I don't think he likes that very much. I think that's why he's refusing."

Well, that's sure not the diagnosis I was expecting, but if that's what Mark was seeing, I was willing to go along with the idea. He suggested that I breathe in and out regularly all the way up to the jump and then exhale as Ashcroft took off. Simple enough, I thought. But it was harder to do than I anticipated. It took several tries to get myself breathing and to get the timing right, but when I did, the feeling was magical. I'd never felt so united with a horse in my life.

During the following days, Ashcroft and I jumped some more, and a pattern became apparent. If I forgot about breathing or breathed very shallowly, he stopped without fail. If I breathed regularly and then exhaled over the jump, he jumped happily and softly every time. Sometimes I couldn't even hear his feet hit the ground as he landed. I was shocked, to say the least, that such a small thing as breathing could affect a horse so profoundly.

When I thought back on it, I had noticed at my first clinic with Mark that he breathed a certain way when he was around the horses. Since he was always wearing a microphone, you could hear it. He breathed evenly, no matter what he was doing. If a rider was struggling, he would almost sigh into the microphone, maybe trying to encourage him to breathe without saying so and thereby adding too many things to his plate. Although I'd noticed it, I had not understood its significance. And it's telling that I did notice—it must have been very different than what I was used to doing and seeing others do around horses.

I never forgot that lesson, needless to say. Ashcroft wouldn't let me. He was most insistent that I keep breathing in everything we did together. I began to wonder how else we could apply breathing to our work with horses, so I began to listen and watch closely at Mark's clinics to discover what other applications there were. By the time I began working for Mark, I believed that breathing was another singular and important key to working well with horses. The lesson I'd learned with Ashcroft was just the tip of a huge iceberg that I would come to know well as my work with Mark progressed.

———⇒◦⇐———

Now, about a year into my apprenticeship with Mark, I feel like I'm just beginning to get a handle on the importance of breathing in our work with horses. When I began teaching with Mark, I asked him, "How do you decide where to start?" I found that when I looked at a horse and rider, I saw so many things I'd like to tweak that I was overwhelmed.

"You can always start with breathing," Mark had answered, and I've remembered that.

When we talk about breathing, we're not talking about the kind of breathing that just gets you by and keeps you from passing out. We're talking about a deep, deliberate, rhythmic, diaphragmatic breath that fills up the lungs and oxygenates the muscles and brain. Most of us don't realize that even in our everyday lives, we don't breathe very well. When we get around our horses, we seem to breathe even less well, to the point that we end up breathing as little as we can and still survive, which is not a help to our horsemanship.

The breathing method that we try to share with clinic participants is similar to the way a horse breathes. A horse breathes rhythmically in a way that moves its rib cage in and out. So that's where we start, with the idea of breathing into the rib cage. To get a feel for this, we might have the riders place their thumbs on their sides at their lowest rib and then breathe in slowly, pushing their thumbs out as their rib cage expands.

There are two other places we can breathe into besides the rib cage, and that's the chest and the belly. Breathing up into the chest is a panic breath of sorts, and it tends to create a very shallow, almost panting type of breathing. A belly breath, on the other hand, is what we might use for meditation or yoga. This breath is deep, but it's not designed to articulate the rib cage and fill up the lungs in an athletic way.

If we can breathe into our ribs, we engage our abdominal muscles, which will support and soften our lower back, which will in turn reduce bracing and bouncing in the saddle and improve our seat.

The next thing we might look at is the depth and duration of that breath. When we coach riders on breathing, we encourage them to inhale long and slow and follow it with a long, slow exhale. We might have riders count how many strides their horses take to each of their inhales and exhales. That number will vary depending on the rider's size, the horse's size and length of stride, the altitude, and any health problems the rider may have.

When I first began to concentrate on my breathing while riding Ashcroft, I found I was lucky to get two or three walking strides to one of my inhales. I was getting two or three to an exhale as well. But the more I worked on it, the more steps I was able to inhale through, until I finally settled at about eight on an inhale and eight or nine on an exhale. A smaller person might get fewer steps than that, a larger person the same or quite a few more steps. I made a point of listening to Mark's breathing while he was riding Mouse at a clinic and wearing a microphone, and I counted thirteen steps at the walk to an inhale. I can't get nearly that many, but I strive to get as many as I comfortably can.

If a rider is holding his breath or isn't breathing well, it creates tightness, making it difficult for his horse to move. If our horse gets scared or concerned, we often hold our breath. That makes it hard for the horse to move under us, just when he's thinking that movement might really be the best thing for him. If we hold our breath, we can become a tight, restrictive, dead weight up there, which might make our horse go from "kind of" concerned to *very* concerned.

As I thought more and more about breathing and helped other people work on it, I began to see why it's so important. Horses do a lot of different kinds of breathing, and how they do it means something to them.

A horse breathes rhythmically and regularly unless something is wrong. A horse that is alarmed snorts explosively through his nose. A horse that is in pain pants or holds its breath. If a horse's breathing gets choppy and erratic, its gaits may as well.

Horses breathe into each other's noses as a greeting. A horse that is sleeping or dozing breathes deeply. Horses hold their breath in order to hear better. That fact makes me think that, in the wild, if one of the horses in a herd changes its breathing, all the horses in the band would notice.

A horse will also exhale with a transition, a stop, a turn, a jump, a lead change, anything that causes him to change his momentum or direction, whether by himself or under saddle with us. So it would be reasonable to presume that if we exhaled too, it might help the horse do his job better. At the very least, it's a small thing we can do to get in sync with his movement or to influence his movement.

After our return from Washington and Oregon, Mark and I were slated for two clinics in De Land, Illinois, outside of Champaign. I'd grown up in the Midwest and hadn't been back to "the motherland," as I irreverently call it, in about ten years. I'd been in the mountains of Colorado so long that I'd almost forgotten the wide prairie, the cornfields, the white farm houses and the red barns of my youth. The drive through central Illinois was a trip back in time for me, a trip back to my roots. I didn't expect to feel so nostalgic about being there again, but I did.

Most of the places we'd traveled to over the year had been new to me, places like central California and Washington and England. But the Midwest felt like home. As we drove through the fallow fields, I thought about how, whether I like it or not, I'm a product of where I grew up. I'm a simple girl, with simple tastes in food, with an appreciation for fertile land and for a good day's work. No matter where I go in life or in the world, those things don't change; they're too deeply rooted. I used to wish that I was more sophisticated or more world-wise, but I've come to see that I'm just a nice girl from the Midwest. And that's okay.

In Illinois, we worked with a woman who wanted to help her horse not throw its head and brace against the bit. Under Mark's tutelage, she began to help her horse soften to the pressure of the bit, and by the time they came down to work some more with me, they had a good start on it.

I worked with Marian and her horse, but something didn't look quite right. I couldn't quite put my finger on what it was. The horse was struggling more than he should, so I went to the old standby, breathing, to see if that would help.

When I asked Marian if she was breathing, she said, "I don't think so." We reviewed how to breathe in a deliberate way, and then I asked her to go back out and see how many walking steps her horse took while she inhaled. Marian started out by getting one to two steps per inhale, but within five minutes she was comfortably up to six or seven. We worked on just getting a feel for breathing better and then returned to asking her horse to soften to the bit.

The struggle was gone. Marian's horse just got soft to the bit, quietly and consistently, as long as Marian was breathing. The horse's stride also increased in length and improved in consistency.

Marian's case is a good example of how breathing can make what we're trying to do either easier on everyone or harder than it needs to be. Marian could have gotten her horse to be soft without focusing on her breathing, but it would have been harder on her and her horse. And it would have taken longer. The change in their work was not earth-shattering, but it was visible to me and palpable to Marian. She was surprised that such a small change could help her horse so much, just as I had been surprised a few years before.

While we were working in Illinois, the wind blew. It blew hard, and it blew all the time, day and night, rattling the doors and roof of the indoor arena. This unsettled a few of the horses, or rather, it unsettled a few of the riders. I found that if I could get them to think about their breathing, they focused on that, instead of worrying about the noises the wind made. Very quickly, the horses that had been a bit tight began to relax, and the horses that were already relaxed began to move better as their riders focused on their breathing.

It isn't just riders who have trouble with breathing. Sometimes even a horse holds its breath, and then it isn't able to move well and can actually build up explosive energy that may come out in unexpected ways. If a horse is holding its breath, the first thing we try to do is get the rider or handler breathing. Often that's enough to get the horse breathing.

It still surprises me to see a horse put his head down and blow his nose as his rider starts to breathe. Each time I see that, it drives home to me how important our breathing is to the horses, even if it's not to us.

When we'd visited England back in July, I'd had a chance to work with a rider on her jumping. Juliet was an experienced rider, riding an experienced horse, and in her lessons with Mark, she'd been working on minimizing her cues so that all she had to do was *think* about what she wanted her horse to do and he would do it. When she asked me to help her with jumping, I was thrilled, and I looked forward to seeing how subtle we could get her cues to be and still have an effect on the horse.

To start with, I had Juliet take some small "X" jumps with her horse while I observed. I noticed that her horse, Jasper, tended to get very close to the jumps before taking off. He didn't hit them, but it's generally accepted that a horse's take-off and landing spots should be about as far from the jump as the jump is tall. This enables the horse to center its arc over the top of the jump, creating smoothness and symmetry in the movement.

The jumps were about eighteen inches high, and Jasper was often taking off only four to six inches from them. This meant that he had to rock way back on his hocks and snap his front end up so he wouldn't hit them. While it's all right for a horse to jump that way, it's not very efficient, and that big rock back onto the hocks wouldn't be necessary if he just took off eighteen inches from the jump. So that made me wonder if Jasper might think that Juliet *wanted* him to do that. Why else would he do something that was physically harder, when the easier option was available?

I watched Juliet and Jasper take about ten jumps and then called her in to discuss what I was seeing.

"Does Jasper usually take off from that close to the jump?" I asked.

"Yes," Juliet answered, "he's always done that with me."

I talked about the inefficiency of that kind of jump and how we might help him be more symmetrical. I proposed we start with Juliet's breathing, as it was the least invasive approach. We didn't want to use a sledgehammer to get the job done if a tweezers would do. I didn't know whether adjusting her breathing would help, as I'd never tried it with this kind of problem. But it made sense that if Juliet were holding her breath, her horse would have trouble coming off the ground.

I asked Juliet to do just what Mark had asked me to do with Ashcroft—breathe in and out regularly all the way to the jump and exhale on the take-off. The first time Juliet tried this, the result was the same: Jasper got right up underneath the jump and had to rock back on his hocks. The second time, Jasper took off where he should, and on the third jump he actually took off too far from the jump. He looked as surprised as we did!

Now, I thought, we had something to work with. At the very least, we'd broken the pattern that Juliet and Jasper had gotten into, and he was offering us different things. At that point, we could shape the behavior into what we needed. Ultimately, what I wanted was for Jasper to sight the jump far enough back in the corner that he could adjust his own stride to get to the jump symmetrically.

It's worth mentioning that this is not what I was taught about how horses should jump, and I struggled with the idea. I was taught that exactly three strides before the jump, the rider must decide where the horse should take off and then make sure that happens. If you watch most riders, they do *something* three strides out from the jump, such as put their leg on or pick up the horse's mouth or sit down. I spent years counting those last three steps aloud to my instructors, "Three, two, one, jump."

Now, that's not a bad thing, as we need to know where we are in relation to the jump. However, with some guidance from Mark, I've come to see that the *horse* actually sights the jump and gauges his steps *much* farther back than that. I've seen horses choose their take-off spot about fifteen steps from the jump. If we're making a decision within the last three steps, that tells me we're *way* behind where the horse is.

An experienced jumping horse sights the jump more than a green horse that still has to grasp the concept of jumping. But as soon as a horse understands the idea, you can feel the horse drawing a bead on the jump before or as you turn, already sorting out its strides. Horses that understand jumping and like it will "hunt" for jumps if there are any in the ring. They're already planning how best to get there.

Since Juliet's horse was an experienced jumping horse, I was guessing that if we let him, he would make the necessary adjustments to get to the jump symmetrically—as long as Juliet didn't get in his way.

After a few more tries with Juliet concentrating on her breathing, Jasper was still taking off a bit erratically. Surprisingly, he wasn't getting too close to the jump, but was taking off just right or too far away. I wanted to see if we could add something subtle to enable Jasper to become more consistent.

I asked Juliet to look up at a big girder with bolts in it between the arena wall and roof when she was four or five strides from the jump. She would need to actually *look* at something up there, the bolts, for instance, and *see* them. Then she could level her eyes again to take the jump.

This is another one of those tiny things Mark had shown me once that make a big difference for some horses. It seems that if we can get the rider to glance up and *see* something, it actually has the effect of lifting the horse over the top of the jump. When I asked Mark why it worked, he said he thinks it lightens the horse and rider somehow so the horse can jump *up* better. Additionally, I think that if the rider can glance up there and focus for a moment, it gets both the horse and rider thinking *UP*. I'd seen this work well with horses that tended to rap jumps with their feet.

So Juliet, good sport that she was, gave it a try. Sure enough, Jasper improved. After six jumps—four that were right where we wanted them and two that were not—I had one more adjustment in mind.

The last thing I wanted to try with Juliet was again based on her breathing. If we're breathing, we should be brace-free and therefore able to feel our horse better. Little movements should telegraph from the horse through to us.

I wanted Juliet to see if, by breathing properly, she could feel Jasper sighting the jump and measuring the distance to the take-off. If she felt that, I encouraged her to be aware of any minute changes he made in his stride and allow them to happen.

This part was really fun for me and Juliet, because she would say when she felt Jasper sight the jump and when she felt an adjustment. When Jasper sighted the jump, sometimes he'd flick his inside ear toward it for a split second, and sometimes there would just be a momentary change in his body. It was so quick that if I blinked at the wrong time, I'd miss it. As we played with this, we found that Jasper consistently sighted the jump about thirteen strides out, and if he made an adjustment in his stride, he did it very shortly thereafter, usually no less than ten or eleven strides from the jump.

Once we'd added this last piece to the puzzle, Juliet and Jasper became very consistent in getting to the jump. We added jumps of different sizes in other places, and they were still consistent. Jasper took off an appropriate distance from the jumps, his arc was centered over it, and he didn't touch any of them. He was soft and happy and willing. He and Juliet were working like true partners. Neither partner was overshadowing the other, and each was doing their part and listening to what the other had to say.

——❖——

The kicker about breathing is that if we decide that it's something that will help our horsemanship, then we really need to practice it away from the horses, in our daily lives. It's one of those things that we can't just instantly do well when we show up to work with our horse. The patterns we've developed in our breathing over the years are deeply ingrained, and our bodies won't give those patterns up without a fight.

There are a myriad of ways to practice breathing during the day. When we're walking, how many steps do we take while we inhale? (It will be about what you'll get on your horse.) When we exert ourselves by picking up a box or opening a car door or tossing our saddle up, do we exhale? When do we hold our breath? Are we even aware that we do?

When I began focusing on breathing in my everyday life, it was tough. I didn't want to do it. It was a bother and just one more item to add to my "to-do" list. But I stuck to it anyway, and I noticed a lot of things. In the beginning, I tended to inhale when I exerted myself instead of exhaling.

I began to notice how I engaged muscles in my shoulders and chest as I inhaled. I could tell I was holding my breath driving Mark's truck and trailer because it didn't take long for my neck and shoulders to ache.

In conversations, I noticed how sometimes I'd run out of breath in the middle of a sentence. Sometimes I couldn't walk and talk at the same time. I'd get to the top of one measly flight of stairs and be out of breath.

In my riding, I discovered that for two decades I'd been holding my breath all the way around a course of jumps. I must have been sneaking little sips of air, but it couldn't have been much. I remembered times when, after two minutes spent jumping a course in the show ring, I came out gasping for breath and felt like I was going to vomit. I had always thought it was nerves, but now I think that it was simply mild asphyxia.

The first time I showed Maggie over fences at a horse show, I knew I was getting somewhere with the breathing thing. After completing our course, I was able to come out of the show ring and have a complete conversation immediately, with no nausea, blue skin, or gasping for breath. I figured that was a vast improvement, so the practice was starting to pay off.

——————————=≫•◆•⇐=——————————

This past year, I've heard Mark say many times to his students all over the world, "The best tool you have to work with horses is right here—it's *you.*"

Breathing is one of those things that is simply about us using our own tools better. It's not complicated or magical, it doesn't require years of study or the purchase of special equipment. But it is profoundly important to our horses.

I am also starting to think that there are layers of awareness and skill in breathing, just as there are in most everything else in horsemanship. When Mark and I returned to the aikido dojo after our trip to Illinois, I got a glimpse of another layer.

We'd just completed a pretty fast-paced class and were all sitting in seiza, a formal sitting posture, for a short, silent meditation at the end of class. As I sat there quietly and breathed, I realized that when my breath went into my body, it felt like it was making a lateral swirl before I exhaled it. It seemed to be going in, then down, then circling up from right to left before being exhaled. I wondered if I could switch the circle of breath so it went longitudinally, front to back. I managed to change the swirl so my breath went in, down, then circled from my back to my front before being exhaled.

I am not sure what importance this has in horsemanship yet, and perhaps it has none. Perhaps I even imagined it. But the horse is a master of subtlety, and if there is significance in it to be found, I trust the horse will find it and show it to me someday.

CONSISTENCY

In December, Mark and I went to England to do the final two clinics of the year. Our year had come full circle in a way—we'd started the year in England and finished it there as well. It seemed to me that maybe that was important somehow, in a way I'd have to think about for a bit.

I love the United Kingdom. I love it that the British call French fries "chips" and that for them chips alone can constitute an acceptable lunch. I love that they call flashlights "torches," halters "headcollars," and trucks "lorries." I love the tartan pattern the hedges make of hillsides, the lane-and-a-half-wide roads, and the vitality of the village high street.

This time, one of the clinics was located in Hampshire, which is, of course, where 19th century literary genius Jane Austen spent much of her life. I'd studied Austen's work extensively in college and was thrilled for the opportunity to spend some time in the landscape that birthed Pride and Prejudice. In the mornings, when mist lay softly on the fields, I imagined that the place looked much the same as it had when Austen lived there. As a devotee of Austen's stories, those mornings were a singular delight.

We did a lot of pub-crawling when we were in England. Most of the clinic venues were in fairly rural areas, and the best chance for a good, quick meal was at one of the myriad of local pubs that dot the countryside. I found out very quickly when I began working with Mark that when you're doing clinics, you covet sleep and plan your non-working hours around it. Without adequate sleep, you get tired easily, lose concentration, and are susceptible to colds and other minor illnesses. So in England, our evenings were usually spent at pubs close to where we were staying.

I'd heard a lot of jokes about English food—about it being bland and overcooked and generally nothing to write home about. But in our three trips to England, I don't think I had what I would call a bad meal. In fact, at one pub I actually had the most wonderful bread I'd ever eaten, a dense, crusty bread with cranberries baked in. Every night we went to that pub, we begged our waitress for cranberry bread, and often she found some in the kitchen, even on nights when they said they weren't serving it.

The pubs in England look and smell and feel just like you think they would. They have dark oak beams, a roaring fire in the fireplace, and lovely old oak-plank tables. They smell of ale and bread and wood smoke. The menu is usually handwritten on a chalkboard. After you make your choice, you place your order with the barman, and a waitress brings your food to the table. Pub food is good, plain food, rarely anything fancy. They usually have steaks, though they sometimes have different names for the cuts of meat than we do in America. There's often lasagna and some kind of meat pie, like chicken and potato or ham with carrots and peas. Chicken is usually available, too, my favorite being a boneless chicken breast topped with ham and local cheddar and served with chips.

After our pub meal, we'd return to the hotel or bed-and-breakfast, where we'd turn in immediately, ready to rise again at 6 A.M. the next day. I love to read before bed, but when I'm clinicing, I'm lucky if I can read a page a night before sleep overtakes me. It can take an eternity to read a book that way.

<hr>

It never fails that (in England particularly) someone will ask Mark about what to do with a horse that is "disrespectful." I've never heard Mark use that word in reference to a horse, and when this question comes up at clinics, he tells folks why.

Mark explains that he's seen a lot of horse in his career; he's seen scared horses and troubled horses and confused horses. He's seen horses that didn't know what to do. But he's never seen a "disrespectful" horse, he says. People often say that a horse that is pushy or runs people over on the ground is "disrespectful." Mark encourages people to look at this the other way around.

Say a horse pushes on a person with its nose, and the person says that's okay. Then the horse rubs its head on that person, and she says that's okay, too. Then finally the horse gives the person a little shove with its head, and she moves out of the way. That horse has been asking all along if it's okay to push on the person and run her over. What's disrespectful about a horse doing what it's been taught is okay, Mark asks. By repeating a behavior a person has said is okay, the horse is actually being very respectful.

When we horse people label a horse or its behavior as "disrespectful," we sometimes use that as a way to blame the horse for what's going on and thereby absolve ourselves of responsibility in the matter. As I see it, the primary responsibility we're absolving ourselves of is a big one—consistency.

Take that pushy horse, for instance. We've been consistent, all right, but not in a productive way. We've seen behavior that can lead to something dangerous, and consistently we've said nothing to the horse about it. Conversely, if we *do* decide to say something to the horse, we're going to have to do it consistently, which means we'll have to pay attention all the time. That takes self-discipline and awareness, among other things. It means saying something to the horse whenever it's required, even if we're working on something else or talking to a friend or in a hurry or just not in the mood. That's a tall order.

The way horses learn is through consistency, for better or worse. Heck, we learn that way, too. If we do something as a one-off and derive a benefit from it, we'll probably try it again. If we benefit again, we'll do it over and over. If we don't benefit, we'll stop doing it. If we sometimes benefit and sometimes don't, we'll probably still hang on to the behavior, since it does benefit us occasionally. We'll at least keep it in mind.

Horses are the same way. They learn very quickly, and the more consistent things are, the faster they learn. Inconsistency seems to bother them quite a bit, and horses that have had a lot of inconsistency in their lives can become pretty troubled. I figure that it must be like standing on quicksand for them; they've got nothing to put their feet down upon confidently.

Consistency is another one of those things that has lots of layers to it, and if we peel one layer off, there's going to be yet another underneath, maybe to infinity, for all I know.

While we were in England, Mark and I had time to do a little sightseeing, which we hadn't been able to do on any of our other trips. We went to Stonehenge and to Salisbury Cathedral, which is accepted as one of the finest examples of Gothic architecture in England. Both Stonehenge and the cathedral were examples of layers of consistency, when I looked at them as such.

Stonehenge was created over many years from 2950 to 1600 B.C. The consistency of those who built it spans many, many generations. Some generations may have gathered data about the movement of the stars and moon and sun; others chose the site and prepared it, while later generations did the construction. The consistency of the concept spanned all those generations.

The pattern of the stones was consistent, although some stones are now missing and others have toppled. But the pattern of concentric circles is absolutely consistent. Their alignment with the stars and sun and moon is absolutely consistent. The placement of the four (now two) "station stones" is consistent.

Salisbury Cathedral, on the other hand, is consistency gone wild. Symbols and shapes are repeated in different sizes, textures, and contexts. Patterns abound inside and out.

The cathedral itself is shaped as a cross. There is a cross on top of the spire, the stone wall surrounding the cathedral features crosses, and stone and wood crosses of every size appear inside and out. The huge nave, where the congregation sits, is formed by massive Gothic arches; the stained glass windows are Gothic arches, as are the doors. The cloister is framed by Gothic arches, and comparatively tiny Gothic arches make up much of the stonework borders and accents.

The cathedral's beauty, it seems to me, comes from its repetition of patterns—its consistency, in other words. It is so huge that there are many opportunities to repeat a pattern. When you look up, you know you'll see a Gothic arch. When you look down, you know you'll see the pattern of the stone floor. Perhaps because the scale is so massive, chaos has to be controlled. Consistency, perhaps, is the source of the cathedral's beauty.

Without consistency, both the Salisbury Cathedral and Stonehenge would be mere piles of rocks. Our eyes and our spirits would find no rest there. But within the patterns, for some reason, we can find respite and refuge. I can't help but wonder if that's how horses view consistency, too—as respite and refuge from chaos.

In England, I had the opportunity to help a student with her horse's leading and ground manners. Trudy and her horse had been together for about two years, and Trudy had recently begun to have trouble with Willow both on the ground and under saddle.

In the ground work, Willow seemed to lack direction. She would wander off if something caught her eye, dragging Trudy with her. She would walk past Trudy, pushing her out of the way with her shoulder. If something startled Willow, she would bump into Trudy as she positioned herself to see better. Trudy said that she simply wanted Willow to "respect her space."

I asked Trudy what her boundaries were while leading Willow.

"What do you mean, 'boundaries'?" Trudy inquired.

"Well," I answered, "how close can she come to you and have that be okay?"

"I don't really know," Trudy said.

And there it was. While Trudy wanted Willow to "respect her space," Trudy herself didn't know where "her space" started and ended, so she was unable to describe that space to Willow. Willow couldn't observe a boundary that didn't exist. Without the consistency of some sort of boundaries, what Trudy and Willow had was chaos.

Trudy and I discussed how she might go about deciding on some rules for Willow on the ground. If Trudy had a few guidelines she could explain to Willow, I suggested, then Willow would know what was expected and could stay out of Trudy's space. It wouldn't be a matter of "respect" in the end; it would be a matter of Willow clearly understanding what the boundaries were.

Trudy settled on a version of the leading guidelines that I often see Mark work on with students: don't run me over; stay an arm's length away; I go, you go; I stop, you stop. With those simple rules in place, Trudy thought she'd feel much safer, and Willow would understand what was expected of her. Those guidelines would pretty much cover any situation that would arise between the two of them on the ground.

The key to teaching Willow those guidelines was consistency, Trudy found. In order for Willow to understand that Trudy wanted her an arm's length away, she had to move Willow out to that boundary every time she breached it. It didn't take long for Willow to understand that there was a line beyond which she was not welcome. There were times when Willow breached the boundary and Trudy didn't notice, and I pointed them out to her, so she could carry through consistently.

Trudy's work with Willow revealed yet another layer of consistency to focus on. Trudy told me that she found it difficult to apply pressure without connecting it with a feeling of being angry or frustrated.

This was fascinating to me, because it was something I'd been thinking about for many months. In our work at Mark's clinics we see both women and men, and I'd begun to notice that we women, more so than men, tend to have difficulty separating pressure from emotion. At times it appeared that if we increased the pressure, we almost couldn't help but increase our emotion, too. I'd had that experience myself with Ashcroft and found myself struggling not to do it with Maggie.

I'd heard Mark say *many* times in the clinic setting that it's essential that we separate our emotions from the work we're doing with horses. I'd given that a lot of thought, since it was something I myself struggled with, and I finally decided that the reason it's so important boils down to consistency.

If we use emotion while we work with a horse, we risk losing our logical thought pattern. Once we lose logical thought, we become inconsistent. Goodness knows how we'll handle a situation if we're not thinking rationally. And then we lose softness as well, because we become reactive rather than responsive.

As women, it seems, we go through much of our lives using as little pressure as we can to get things done. But then we get angry or frustrated or annoyed, and as the emotion increases, so does the pressure. Now we're in a mess, and we do things we later regret.

In Trudy's case, we had the opportunity to talk about separating our emotions from our work. There was no need for Trudy to become annoyed or frustrated with Willow, as I saw it. If Trudy could see their new ground work guidelines as "just business," rather than something personal between them, then perhaps she wouldn't get angry. Those guidelines weren't there to make Willow miserable or to put Trudy on some pedestal of hierarchy between them; they were there simply to keep Trudy safe.

As long as Trudy was safe, she could take good care of Willow, and Willow would benefit in ways she couldn't possibly know. If Trudy got hurt because of Willow, Willow would suffer in ways she also couldn't possibly know. If Trudy looked at her work with Willow in that context—helping Willow would keep both of them safe—then maybe she could take the emotion out of it.

Trudy practiced her new guidelines for the rest of the clinic, focusing on being consistent with Willow in different environments and situations. The key to Trudy's work was consistency—those guidelines couldn't change situationally or on a whim. Willow needed to know where the boundaries were so that she could be confident and feel good about her work with Trudy.

—=◆◇◆=—

I grew up using a lot of emotion when I worked with horses. It was okay, as far as I knew, to use anger and frustration, so I did. I can remember being so angry with Ashcroft in the beginning that I couldn't even see straight. I knew it wasn't necessarily "good horsemanship" to get so angry, but I didn't really know what else to do.

I'd been attending Mark's clinics for four or five years when I finally began to peel off that layer of understanding about emotional consistency. I was riding Ashcroft in a clinic I was sponsoring, and we were in an indoor arena. Ashcroft was spooky that day for whatever reason, and we had a hard time maintaining a nice, soft trot. He felt tight and wound up, and I became frustrated with him very quickly. How long had I been at this, and I still had trouble maintaining a rideable trot!

Then an idea struck me. What if I at least *acted* like I wasn't frustrated? I didn't think I could actually manage to not *be* frustrated, but I thought maybe I could fake it long enough to see what would happen. So that's what I did, right there in the clinic. I faked it. I pretended I wasn't frustrated. I asked myself, *What would I do right now if I wasn't frustrated?* Then I did it.

Miracles of miracles, as I faked being not frustrated, Ashcroft softened up and calmed down. In no time at all, I had the soft, rideable trot I'd been looking for. Ideally, I don't want to fake feeling a certain way, because my horse knows when I'm faking it. I'm sure Ashcroft knew that day I was faking it. But he gave me credit for it anyway, which told me that I was at least moving in the right direction.

That experiment opened up a whole vista for me of what might be possible if I could indeed take emotion—and the inconsistency it created—out of my work. I still don't have that licked by a long shot, but I'm a lot further along now. As I get a handle on one layer of this, another is revealed, and I get back to work on it.

In March when Mark and I picked up Maggie, I knew that she'd have some things to teach me. I didn't know what those things would be, of course, because I didn't know her well. I looked forward to getting to know her and learning what she was all about.

Due to our schedule, I didn't actually start working with Maggie until about June, when we were doing the summer clinics. I decided to use Maggie at clinics right away to see what she thought of them.

Maggie approached her job of being a clinic horse with what I would almost call coolness. She didn't *not* like it, but she wasn't thrilled with it either. She was easy to catch each morning and she did her job well all day. She was fine being in close contact with unfamiliar horses, she stood tied by her bridle to the fence if I needed her to, and she demonstrated any little thing I needed her to. I found that if I left her somewhere, she kept an eye on me, and if she could, she followed me.

As we started the clinics, we also started working cattle, which I didn't know if she'd done before. This, too, she approached coolly. She was willing to go out there and push on the cows, giving them a little nip if needed, to do her part in getting the cattle where they needed to go. But she didn't act like some horses that just can't wait to get out there and go to work on the cattle.

About the same time, we also started jumping. This she did with the same composure I'd seen in our other pursuits. She didn't seem to mind jumping, but she wasn't enthusiastic about it either. She behaved the same way at her first horse shows and the same way on her first Rocky Mountain trail ride—always slightly cool, always predictable.

I started to think about all this, because Maggie was behaving in a way that was very different from how Ashcroft behaves. Ashcroft *loves* to jump. He just lights up when there are jumps around. Anyone can tell that he has a real passion for it. Heck, if he were turned out in an area with jumps, he'd jump them on his own just for fun!

I suppose that I was expecting to see something of the same passion in Maggie at some point. I began to wonder if I just hadn't yet offered her the one pursuit that would light her up. I wondered if I needed to try some new disciplines that I wasn't familiar with so she could find her "niche."

Then something occurred to me. Perhaps Maggie was walking the proverbial middle line. I'd heard Mark say that in his life and in his work, he tries to stay in the middle emotionally—neither soaring high as a kite nor dipping into deep depression. That way, if something important comes along, he can evaluate it from the middle and respond accordingly.

What I was seeing with Maggie was that she neither soared sky high nor dragged her feet in the dirt in dejection. She appeared to do most everything from the middle. I'd seen it as "coolness," but perhaps it was simply the lack of intense emotion. That meant that she didn't light up like Ashcroft, but it also meant that I could count on her coming to whatever job I asked of her much the same way every time. There is something to be said for that kind of consistency.

⟫•◈•⟪

I know that Mark offers his horses layers of consistency that I haven't yet grasped. I also know that I struggle with being consistent—even on the layers that I *do* understand. Mark's consistency is reflected in his horses' consistency. They behave pretty much the same way pretty much all the time. And if you look, you can see that they derive a deep confidence from Mark's consistency.

I think there are certain kinds of consistency that horses really appreciate, and one is our ability to remove emotion from our work with them. Looking back, I can see that when I used to work with horses by relying on my emotions, those horses always appeared to be "waiting for the other shoe to drop." They never knew, from one day to the next, what frame of mind I'd be in or why I'd do what I did with them.

These days, it makes sense that I had trouble catching Ashcroft in the beginning. My work with him had been governed by the emotions of anger and frustration. The easiest way for him to deal with that was to avoid dealing with it at all, if he could.

Being emotionally consistent requires us to be able to check our emotions at the gate, so to speak. It's not really the horse's responsibility to sort through all our complicated motivations and feelings to decipher if there's a cue meant for him in there somewhere.

⟫•◈•⟪

Another kind of consistency that I see vividly in Mark's work is that he always offers the softest cue first, and the horse can count on that. The horse may not respond to that small cue, but it appears to be really important to horses that it comes first.

This is one of those things that I don't quite understand the full depth of yet. While we were in England that last time, Mark did quite a few trailer-loading sessions. Each horse he worked with had a different reason for not loading promptly, and Mark handled each loading session a bit differently. What was consistent was that Mark first offered a small cue with the least amount of pressure he could.

Now, he wasn't always able to get the job done with that small cue. But he consistently started soft and ended soft. Sometimes the cues were more emphatic in the middle of the session, depending on what the horse offered back. However, he always offered that small cue first. Of course, Mark was doing more than simply offering a cue; he was also being soft, being confident, thinking outside the box, and so on. But in the trailer-loading situations, when those horses were worried in the first place, they really needed the kind of consistency Mark could offer.

⁂

Like so much else, consistency is one of those things that we either practice or we don't. We can't very well live our lives in chaos and then expect to approach our horses with serenity and composure. Whatever consistency we want to take to our horses, we need to practice in life.

A friend of mine studied with Mark a few times, and one of the things she worked on was stopping her older horse promptly. She worked at this in a clinic, and it did improve. A couple months later, I saw her in a local bakery and asked after herself and her horse. Interestingly, she said that since she'd worked on her stops with her horse at the clinic, she'd noticed that she rarely stopped her truck fully when driving. The way she stopped her truck, she said, was just how she stopped her horse. Once she began stopping properly in her truck, her horse's stops had improved as well.

I know in life, at least in my life, it's darned difficult to be consistent. Again, it's just not one of those things that we necessarily value in our culture. But if we could actually be consistent in life, if we could drive consistently, if we could move at a consistent pace through our day, stay true to our word, maybe uphold our own values consistently, well, I wonder what kind of effect that would have on our horsemanship.

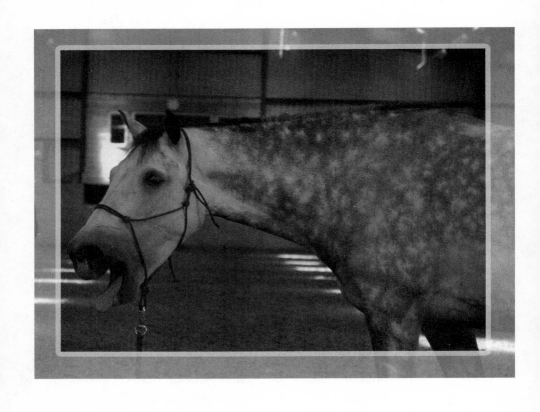

SIMPLICITY

Quite a few years ago Ashcroft became terribly ill with some form of colitis, which basically meant his intestines were inflamed. Practically, it meant he was deathly ill and had about a ten percent chance of survival. But survive he did, thanks to dozens of liters of fluids, lots of injections of fancy drugs, and his own will to fight—with which I was very familiar.

Ashcroft was in intensive care in the horse hospital for a week, and when he was released, I turned him right back out in his two-acre paddock with his friends at the boarding stable, because I was sure he'd missed them.

On the second day after his release, I went out to give him his medication and take his temperature and found that he was moving very strangely. He couldn't walk straight forward. Instead, he kind of crabbed sideways with tiny little steps. He got where he wanted to go, but it looked pretty horrible. I had the barn manager look at him, and we agreed that the problem might be neurological. So off I went to call the vet again.

When he arrived, the vet watched Ashcroft move around and then examined him, doing a couple of simple neurological tests.

"I think he's just sore," was his pronouncement.

"It's not neurological?" I asked.

"Let's just take the simplest solution for now. You know ... Ockham's razor."

Ockham's razor, my vet explained, is a principle that advises simplicity in scientific inquiry. It is often restated as, the simple solution is most often the correct solution. My vet used the principle as a starting place in a lot of his cases.

Ashcroft had been a pincushion for a week, receiving injections in the

111

muscles of his neck, chest, and haunches every day in the hospital, not to mention the IV catheter inserted in his neck. It made sense that he would be sore enough to cause him to move strangely. The vet prescribed massage therapy. I got the horse masseuse out to see him, and within a day or two, Ashcroft was much better.

I didn't give Ockham's razor much more thought until I began working with Mark, although this time the idea was called "keep it simple." When I looked, I saw common threads running through everything Mark did, both in his work with horses and in his life. One of those threads was certainly "keep it simple." It wore different guises in different situations, but it was there all the same. I could see it in the idea of using as little tack and equipment as possible with the horses and in grouping all the family's errands into one trip to town. That's keeping it simple.

<hr>

William of Ockham, a 14th Century English Franciscan friar, logician, and philosopher, is most famous for the principle that bears his name, which is also known as the principle of parsimony or the law of economy. This was expressed as, *Pluralitas non est ponenda sine necessitate.* Translated from Latin it means, "Multiples should not be used if not needed."

In practice it is often used to mean, "Given two equally productive theories, choose the simpler." Or, as students are taught in some medical schools, "When you hear hoof beats, think horses, not zebras."

Also attributed to Ockham is this phrase, *Frustra fit per plura quod potest fieri per pauciora.* That means, "It is pointless to do with more what can be done with less."

There was the golden thread, the thread that tied together everything I'd learned over the past year working with Mark: "It is pointless to do with more what can be done with less." This single idea was the one that all the others were in aid of. Even if we could use none of the other ideas, *this* was an idea we could start with.

<hr>

Ironically, although it appears that it should be easier to simplify than to multiply, that isn't always the case. As a matter of fact, many of us did start with simplicity, when we were kids. As kids, we just rode. We rode and rode and rode, and we got our horses to do things we never should've been able to get them to do because we hadn't yet "learned" how to train them. Before I'd ever had riding lessons that encompassed the subjects, I was jumping picnic tables with my horse, doing flying lead changes, and standing her up in perfect halter poses. And it wasn't just me; all my friends could do things they hadn't been taught how to do.

We didn't agonize about it or look it up in books and magazines (or on the internet if we'd had it), we just went out and tried stuff. If it didn't work, we tried something else. If we fell off, we got back on. In a nutshell, we kept it simple, really simple.

But somewhere along the way, that simplicity was lost. I read lots of books, looked at lots of catalogs, and took a lot of lessons. And I grew up, of course. Things got quite a bit more complicated. Riding wasn't just riding anymore, it was RIDING. Instead of me and my horse and a saddle and bridle, it was me and my horse and martingales and draw reins and longe lines and side reins and spurs and sticks. My collection of bits swelled from one to dozens. Whatever the latest, greatest piece of equipment was, I had to have it. Whoever the latest, greatest trainer was, I had to work with him or her. The days of jumping picnic tables faded far behind me. I was doing with more what could be done, and *had* been done, with much less.

The thing was, at the time, I thought that more was actually better. Maybe it was the culture I was a part of, maybe it was just a routine part of growing up, I don't know. But looking back, it seems like things got really complicated really fast. One minute I was giggling my way through a tandem bareback class at a local horse show, and the next moment I was buried under a mountain of information and opinions.

⋙◆⋘

We see this kind of information overload at Mark's clinics. Now, don't get me wrong. Sometimes things truly are complicated. If that's the case, we see what we can do to sort things out. But much of the time, things could be pretty simple if we'd let them.

Take cues, for instance. It seems to me that spectators at Mark's clinics spend more time asking Mark why he's *not* doing what he's not doing than they spend asking him why he *is* doing what he's doing. There's nothing wrong with that, of course. I'm glad they're asking. But it tells you something about what they're thinking and what their expectations are.

People often ask why Mark isn't instructing his students to use more cues. I think they're basically asking why Mark isn't teaching the cues that are in "The Book," whatever book that is. Mark usually answers that he's using one or two cues and not more because they may not need more in that situation. If they do, they can always add more.

Frustra fit per plura quod potest fieri per pauciora. Heck, it's Ockham again. "It is pointless to do with more what can be done with less."

Let's look at backing. Typically we'll begin by asking a student to back up his horse by simply giving a rein cue. Often an auditor will ask if the rider should sit back and/or put some leg on as well. Now, we could do all those things at once, but if the horse *can* back up with just one cue, why would we add those others? At its simplest, all we're doing is putting a cue to a thing the horse can already do out in the pasture by itself. You'd think we could do that with a minimum of cues.

I'm not quite sure why we horse people are so dedicated to giving lots and lots of cues. Maybe it makes us feel smarter than the horse or smarter than other riders; maybe we just can't stand for something like riding to be simple. This is yet another of those contradictions in our horsemanship that we indulge ourselves in. We long for quiet trail rides and smooth, flawless lead changes. Then we spend a whole lot of time tying ourselves in knots trying to get there. I'm thinking that those knots we get ourselves in just take the fun right out of this.

———≫◦≪———

Riders and spectators also ask Mark why he's not working on other things that a horse or rider might be doing incorrectly. Take a rider who has come to work on getting more impulsion with his horse. Mark starts helping him with it, and in a little while, someone in the audience says, "But that horse is falling in. Aren't you going to do something about it?"

Usually Mark's answer runs along the lines of, "That's not what we're working on right now. Right now, we're working on impulsion."

We all do this, in our horsemanship and in our lives, to some extent. We get working on one thing and then something else catches our eye, and there we go, off on that bunny trail, just like that. Often, we never finish the thing we originally set out to do. We're back to Ockham's razor, "Multiples should not be used if not needed."

It's so easy for us to multiply and multiply and multiply, especially with horses for some reason. We all have wish lists for our horses that are half a mile long. We want our horse quiet and responsive and straight and energetic and on the correct lead with his head in a certain place and his feet landing a certain way with a particular shape to his body. But you know, in the end, it's just a canter. It's a canter like I used to do when I was twelve years old alongside the road by my friend Jenny's house when I rode her gray Arabian.

What if we could work with our horse in such a way that when we put it away at the end of the day, the horse could list *exactly* what we worked on that day? We humans like to have things that clear. "I went to work today and moved 225 widgets from point A to point B." If I can say that, I know what I did.

Sometimes, I think our horses might be saying something more like, "Well, I started out putting some widgets over there, but then I cleaned a window because it was dirty. After that, I stood for a while, and then I stacked some boxes."

It might be helpful for me to keep that in mind, that I'd really like my horse to know what we did any given day. If I can keep things that clear, I think he might get so he feels pretty good about our work.

Being on the road is a simple life and it isn't. It's simple because there's so much you can't do anything about. You can't do anything about weather or traffic jams or closed roads or people dropping out of clinics because a relative is sick. It's not so simple in that there's a lot of planning that goes into the business itself and each trip individually.

When we're not on the road, life at home is simple and it isn't. It's simple because there aren't any clinics to deal with. But being home between clinics is not simple, like a vacation; it's time when other important things are attended to. For Mark, being home means answering e-mails and going to his sons' football games, basketball games, and track meets. It means buying hay, stacking hay, getting horses trimmed or shod, and having maintenance done on the truck and trailer. There are horses to feed every day and pens to clean.

Mark might spend his time at home sitting at the dining room table, writing his next book. He might spend a weekend at an auction, looking for nice prospects to buy and sell. He might help his buddies out at the big ranch in town, branding or moving cattle or fixing fence. Then there are book signings, taking stacks of envelopes full of books and DVDs to the post office, and attending and teaching aikido classes.

My life off the road is simpler than Mark's in that it still revolves mostly around horses, and I don't have a family. When I'm home, I ride as much as I can and go to horse shows, if the scheduling is right. I teach some local students, and I catch up with paying bills, doing my banking, and opening mail. I catch up with friends via the phone and email. I help stack hay, get the horses trimmed or shod, and do the daily chores—anything that needs done. I go to every aikido class I can. I get my hair cut and go to the dentist and the doctor.

Living mostly on the road is something many people never do in their lifetimes. It's another one of those things that could be really complicated if we let it. In the end, we're just going around helping people with their horses. Then we go home, catch up on that part of our lives, and do it all over again.

Besides adding unneeded cues and working on too many things at once, another thing I think we do that adds unnecessarily to what's already going on is non-productive anthropomorphizing. Now, I believe that horses have emotions, and I believe that as horsemen, part of what we need to do is *work* with the horse's emotions. We need to be able to see when a horse is scared or troubled or when he just needs a moment to think or take a breather. That's productive, because in attributing those emotions or traits to the horse, we're helping the horse make progress.

There are times, though, when we're needlessly complicating things and preventing progress by attributing a human emotion or trait to a horse. For instance, when any horse is trying to learn a new skill, he generally offers all the things he already knows before he tries something new. That's natural. People do it too, and it's just part of learning. But sometimes when the horse keeps offering what he already knows over and over, we say, "See, he hates doing this!"

That's all it takes to shut down the learning process. Perhaps what the horse is feeling isn't so much "hate" as "confusion," which is very different. Confusion is a pretty neutral emotion. But "hate" is a strong word that reflects a negative feeling.

In a case like this, we're over-complicating the situation by attributing a feeling to the horse that he may not feel at all. We risk getting so worried that our horse hates the work and hates us that he'll end up standing out there in the pasture while we take up needlepoint.

I've seen this happen often when a horse stomps his foot while a rider is working on something.

"Oh, no," the rider might say, "now he's mad!"

Maybe. But he might just have needed to stomp his foot; that's the simpler explanation. If we view that foot stomp as a signal that the world is coming to an end, then it may well just do that. On the other hand, if we just accept that the horse needed to stomp his foot and get on with our work, we might just get where we want to go.

Attempting to simplify my work with horses in this way has been very difficult for me. I spent a lot of time in the beginning of my work with Ashcroft trying to watch closely for his "tries," and in the process, I think I ended up taking anthropomorphizing just a bit too far. That's not a bad thing, necessarily. It was an important stage I needed to go through in my horsemanship, but it did mean that there were days I wondered what the heck I was doing sitting there psychoanalyzing things when I could have been riding.

With the advent of the internet, multiplying factors exponentially and complicating situations needlessly is getting easier and easier to do. We sometimes hear it called the "paralysis of analysis."

I've been on a few horsemanship-oriented e-mail chat groups in my time, and I've noticed something about them. Someone writes in with a fairly simple question and weeks and weeks of analysis and discussion follow. Now, there's nothing wrong with that, because by definition that's the purpose of an e-mail *discussion* group.

When I think about how some of those groups work and how Ockham's razor works, I wonder if what we were doing was multiplying factors enthusiastically and getting things just about as complicated as we could. It seems like we did a lot more adding of factors than subtracting of factors. I wonder if, in our zeal to have an exciting discussion, the original question and the needs of the person who asked it got lost. The simplest thing to do would have been to keep the questioner's best interests in mind.

I look at something like that and I ask myself if the energy that's being put into it is proportional to the benefit being reaped on the other end. Maybe it is. Maybe it isn't. But it seems to me like it should be.

A friend of mine who attends Mark's clinics annually related this story to me. She'd asked Mark for help with some trouble she was having with her horse when he was loose in his pen. She would go in to doctor a cut or whatever, and he would move off. She was concerned that this meant her horse didn't like her or didn't trust her leadership. She asked Mark what she should do about it.

Mark said, "Well ... you could put a halter on him."

—♦—

Simplicity is something I see in aikido, as well. In the dojo, simplicity starts with the belt system. I'm a lower belt, while Mark is a much higher belt. The shihan is the head teacher, the owner of the dojo, and the top guy. There is never any question in the dojo as to where people fall in the heirarchy. All we've got to do is look at their belts.

Another thing that's simple about aikido is movement. When I was observing aikido classes, I thought it looked very complicated. The first thing I learned was the "kata," all the basic physical movements of the art, organized into a prescribed form that a student memorizes and then practices. Suddenly, those movements I saw everyone else doing made a lot more sense because, within them, I could see the elements of the kata. All the seemingly elaborate movements were, at their heart, moves from the kata. So what looked impossibly complicated to me at first still looked complicated but now seemed *possible*, with knowledge of the simple kata.

It's the same with our horsemanship, really. When we practice the basics, the simple stuff, we're practicing the "big stuff" at the same time. The very basics of riding horses are go, stop, back up, turn left, and turn right. Every other thing we do is a version of those basics. The reiner's spin is a version of "turn left" or "turn right." The dressage rider's canter pirouette is a version of "go" and "turn left" or "turn right." Jumping is a version of "go." Those elements form the basis of everything we'll need in order to do whatever it is we want to do with our horses.

If we can get the simple stuff working really well, then it's relatively easy to add speed or some other sort of wrinkle. It's just like aikido; if we've got that kata working well, then it's not a big step to do a maneuver with someone holding onto us. We have a base from which to build.

In aikido, simplicity is one of those golden threads that ties everything together. If a move gets a bit troublesome, the best way I've found to help myself along with it is to simplify. It's the same with horsemanship. When I look at any situation and try first to simplify things, I'm more likely to untie knots than make more knots.

———※·◇·※———

Mark discusses with students a concept that's based on his aikido training. It's the idea of one's mind being like "still water." If a body of water is still, it's like a mirror. It can reflect the scene around it very accurately. But if the water's surface is disturbed, the image it reflects is distorted or even unidentifiable.

Mark suggests that we try to approach our work with horses with a "mind like still water," so we can see clearly what is around us. Many of us tend to throw pebbles in our water—"Oh, the neighbor's dog is out." Plunk, there goes a pebble into that still pond, and now the ripples are undulating out, breaking up the reflection in the mirror.

Our self-doubts can also throw pebbles in the water—"I'll never get this." Plunk, there goes another pebble. Other people can throw pebbles in the water—"Are you done yet? I need the round pen!" Plunk, plunk. If we let our minds wander like that while we're working with our horses, we risk becoming unclear, both with ourselves and with our horses.

If we can keep a "mind like still water," we can see and feel what the horse does when he does it and understand it for what it is, without a lot of static breaking up the picture. We can be "in the moment" with the horse because we're there, involved in what's going on between us, rather than the horse being involved in the work while we're somewhere else mentally.

Within the idea of "mind like still water" is simplicity, the concept of not multiplying things needlessly. When we're working with our horse, we should be working with our horse, not making grocery lists or planning tonight's party or going over how our co-worker got the promotion we wanted. If we do that, we're multiplying the things our mind has to do, and those things have nothing to do with the horse. The horse doesn't care about any of those things. What he does care about, I think, is clarity—understanding what we want and succeeding at it.

Being clear is something we can practice in life so we can take it to our horsemanship. How often are we misunderstood by others? How often do we not get what we need because we don't ask clearly? If we look at being clear from the standpoint of Ockham's razor, it is easier to be clear than it is to be muddled. It's more efficient to be clear. If we're clear, we're getting things done with as little as possible.

⟫⟪

I'm not sure why we horsemen like to complicate things so much. I've done it and I still do it, and I really don't know why. I can remember vividly those days as a kid just fooling around with horses. Everything seemed so easy, and more than that, there was *joy* in the work. I can remember being overtaken by fits of giggles and going home from lessons giving my mother an excited play-by-play recitation of everything that went on.

Then I grew up, and suddenly a canter wasn't a canter, it was a CANTER, and a jump wasn't just a jump, it was a JUMP. Somehow, the joy had seeped out of it. I quit riding once for seven months because of that— because it wasn't fun anymore. Working with horses had become a chore. In the end, I couldn't stay away, of course, but I knew I had to find joy in the work or it wasn't worth it.

I think there's something to be said for the way kids ride and work with horses. They do it simply. They do it joyfully. If something doesn't work, they try something else. They *feel* rather than think. They see the good. They're not afraid to look silly. They're creative. They trust their intuition. They giggle and shout once in a while. I'm starting to think that those simple things are the important things when it comes to working with horses.

We can deconstruct what we do with our horses and analyze it and pick it apart, and then put it back together again, but in the end, it's still just working with a horse. We're not talking about quantum physics or cold fusion here; it's just working with a horse. Each of us possesses all the tools we need to work with horses successfully. We carry those tools wherever we go, and we have since we were born. Sure, we'll get stuck, especially if we're going places we haven't gone before. That's just part of the deal.

But I'm thinking that if we can do nothing else as we go along with our horses, we can keep it simple, and we'll have a touchstone—a place to start. Heck, that goes for life as well. I'm thinking that Ockham was a wise man.

Frustra fit per plura quod potest fieri per pauciora.

"It is pointless to do with more what can be done with less."

11

HOPE

Mark and I wrapped up the year's schedule with the two clinics in England in early December and then flew home. I was home for a week and then flew by myself to the Hawaiian island of Kauai, where I planned to spend Christmas. I would hike and read and wear tank tops while it was snowing back home. It's funny, but with all the travel we'd done that year, when I had a vacation coming, I chose ... to travel.

One of the first things I did when I got to Kauai was look up a friend, David Carswell. I'd met David years ago, through a mutual friend in Colorado. He is an excellent horseman in his own right, and on Kauai he and his wife run a working ranch and very successful adventure outfitting company, which offers horseback rides, among many other things.

After a visit to his office and a couple of false starts, I caught up with David at his stable where we pulled a couple of upturned pails into the shade to "talk story," as they say there, or "catch up" as we'd say on the mainland. The trade winds drifted in lazily from the ocean, and on the horizon the sky and the sea met in a wash of blue. We were literally across the world from where I'd been only a few weeks earlier, England. Amazing.

David and I talked for a while about this and that, just what had gone on in our lives and businesses since we'd last seen each other a few years previously. Then David asked, "So, what do you think is the most important thing you learned while working with Mark this year?"

I wasn't prepared for the question. You'd think I would be, it being the end of the year and all, but I fell silent for quite a while. The answer I eventually gave him is different from the answer I'll give now. And in another year, or in ten years, it might well be different again.

123

⟫◆⟪

Last summer Mark and I were sitting at a picnic table with the participants of one of the clinics in Loveland. As homework the previous evening, we'd asked the students to come prepared to tell us about something they felt they practiced in their lives and then brought to their horse work. When we'd gone around the table and all the students had given their answers, one of the students asked Mark what *he* practiced in life and brought to his horse work.

He answered, "I think I bring hope. I always believe things will work out."

Hope. Simple as that. That cut right to the quick, for me at least. Do I bring hope or despair to my life and my work? Which do I practice? It's a choice we make, either way.

Mark chooses to bring hope to everything he does. Sometimes that's a hard thing to do; it can be brutally hard, in fact. Despair is a sneaky thing. It can creep in surreptitiously, and before we know it, we're basing our decisions on the belief that things *won't* work out.

I think it takes a lot of courage to be hopeful. I didn't know that when I started working for Mark. I just thought some people are hopeful and positive and some people aren't. I saw myself as one of the ones who isn't. But now I see that it wasn't hopefulness I lacked, it was the *courage* to be hopeful. It was easier to be jaded and cynical and pessimistic because that didn't take any courage.

I'd never thought of myself as a particularly cowardly person. My mother had raised me to be confident and secure. But somewhere along the way, I think life knocked me around just a little bit, and I started to believe that no matter what I did, no matter how well I lived, maybe things *wouldn't* work out in the end.

What bothered me about that philosophy was that it showed up in my horsemanship. As long as I was willing to relinquish hope, my horses would not be the best they could be. If I abandoned hope, even on the most insignificant level, what did I have to offer students, whether horse or human?

⟫◆⟪

Mark and I would both agree that I haven't been an easy student to teach—either as a clinic participant or as an apprentice. But I can see that Mark never gave up hope that I would come through and succeed at whatever it was, be it a better lead change or becoming a good teacher.

At first, Mark's hope was sometimes all that carried us through, but as time went on, I can see that he expected me to provide my own hope, as it were. And of all the things I've done in this job, that has been perhaps the hardest for me to do.

The way that Mark works with horses, and Walter Pruitt before him I expect, is based not on a set of techniques or skills, but on a philosophy, a simple collection of ideas. The good thing is that within that set of ideas, there is a lot of flexibility for individuality, adaptation, and independence. The not-so-good thing is that there isn't a point at which you've clearly succeeded in learning the material. There is no graduation, no diploma, no overt sign that you have "arrived."

Instead, there is the living of that simple collection of ideas: listen to what the horse has to say, think creatively, work *with* the horse. These ideas apply to life as well, and since I will get good at what I practice, it's important that I be able to practice those ideas in life as well as in horsemanship.

As my year with Mark progressed, I certainly learned to listen better to what horses have to say. I found that I also listened to people more intently and interrupted less. At clinics I noticed that sometimes students would be slightly tongue-tied during their session with Mark, maybe because he's the guy who's written all the books and whom they've waited so long and wanted so much to work with. But occasionally when someone came down to work with me, the floodgates would open, and they would talk and talk and talk. The best thing I could do, I figured, was listen. I began the year thinking my job was to instruct, but really, my job was to support Mark's work in whatever way I could. Sometimes that meant listening while people talked, rather than instructing them.

Wherever we are, the people and even the things around us have something to say. The movies we see, the music we listen to, and the books we read have something to say. We can either let that stuff in, or we can shut it out, depending on how useful or constructive it is. What we don't want to do, if we can help it, is just plain *miss* what people and things have to say.

We have something to say, too. I have something to say, and not only do I want to consider carefully what that is so that it has integrity and honors my teachers, I also want to make sure it's heard. The best way to be heard, I've discovered, is to talk only when I have something important to say. The less we talk, I think, the more we're actually listened to.

Thinking creatively in life, another idea important to Mark, can be a tough challenge, as we all get stuck in patterns that work for us. Those patterns work for us until they don't work for us anymore, if you see what I mean. We drive the same way to the same places, we order the same kinds of foods when we eat out, we use the same defense mechanisms, and we try hard to keep our thinking the same. But if we can simply think a bit creatively, we sometimes see opportunities and solutions that weren't obvious before.

Shortly after I began working for Mark, I started saving the little messages that I got in fortune cookies at Chinese restaurants. It could be coincidence, of course, but an inordinate number of my fortunes seemed to say one version or another of, "Now is a good time to try something new."

Heck, I figured, I had nothing to lose. I was already trying something new by working full-time as an apprentice for an internationally respected clinician. So I took that advice to heart. At the very least, I decided it might help me think a little differently. I started doing tai chi, then aikido. I made new friends. I tried new styles of clothes. I read different books than I was used to and listened to different music. At restaurants I made a point of ordering food that was a bit off the beaten path for me.

I found out that the sky didn't fall on me. Sure, sometimes the new things weren't as good as the old things, but it wasn't a tragedy or a disaster. At the very least, after trying something new and finding I preferred the old, I knew *why* I preferred what I preferred. By getting out of my own box, I discovered new ways of doing things, new friends, new ideas, and good things all around me that I hadn't seen but had always been there. It's funny how sometimes we can't see the multitude of things around us because we're so focused on the one thing with which we're familiar.

Working *with* what's around us is also very difficult in life and in horse work, in part because we're culturally educated to work *against* from a very young age. We're taught to "Look out for #1," "Win at all costs," and "Make the sale, no matter what."

All that's fine and good, but I wonder how much more efficiently we could do those same things by working *with* instead of *against*.

Our lives are kind of like rivers. We can either be the water flowing or the boulder in the middle of the river that the water has to go around. If we're that boulder, we cause ripples and whitewater and noise and foam. If we're the water, one way or another we're going to reach sea level, where we belong.

⋙◆⋘

I know full well that these ideas are great stuff, if we have the powers of a superhero and the tolerance and serenity of a Buddhist monk. And there's a part of me that really wants to believe that it's all possible. That's the hopeful part of me.

Working with Mark showed me that we don't start where we end up, and we shouldn't expect to. There were times when I wished that I was better than I was, or farther along than I was, or just plain *not* the way I was. But the fact of the matter is, whatever we're doing, it's a process. Horsemanship is a process. Life is a process. If we spend too much time wishing we were somewhere or someone else, we won't be able to make the most of where or who we actually *are*.

I began to see that these things are not forever. Whatever stage we're at in whatever process, it's not forever. Things will change if we let them. It's actually when we feel like we're struggling or that nothing is happening that the learning is taking place. The "breakthrough" moment is the culmination of the learning, not the learning itself.

In all of this I can find comfort. I'm not as good at much of anything that I do as I would like to be someday, but that's okay. As long as I'm doing the best I can with what I've got available to me at the time, then I can sleep at night. That's really all we can ask of ourselves.

And it's the same for horses. They're all in a process of one sort or another. They're in a certain place on the road. All we can ask is that they do the best they can with what they've got available to them at that point in time. Wherever they are right now, they won't be there forever. But maybe where they are at this moment is exactly where they're supposed to be, even if it doesn't quite fit in with our plans.

The first time I did a clinic with Mark in Scotland, we stayed in a beautiful cottage alongside a pasture full of sheep, with high hills in the distance. Many evenings, after the clinic, Mark and I would find our way to the sitting room where there would be cheese and fruit laid out, and we'd talk about the day. We didn't get to do that at most clinics, so those days were very memorable for me. But they were fleeting. The setting changed, that clinic ended. That's not a bad thing, that's just how things work.

That's how I've come to look at horse showing. It's transitory. I have about two minutes to construct a thing of beauty for the judge and the audience who is there, and then it's gone. It evaporates, and all that's left is the memory of it. Now, that's a good thing if that performance wasn't the greatest. It's not so good if it was the performance of a lifetime and I'd like to see or feel it again.

But we can't have it both ways. We can't keep only the good and abandon the not-so-good. It's just as well that we can't keep a lot of this stuff, because if we could, we'd have no reason to hope to do it again or see it again or feel it again. It's the hope of having that magic moment on a horse's back that keeps me climbing up there day after day, just like it's that hope of turning in an exceptional round that keeps me going to the horse shows. Whether it happens or not is almost not the point, the point is that the hope for it exists.

At Mark's clinics, we see a lot of people in search of hope. Maybe it's the hope that they can get along better with their horses, or the hope that they can get through a spot that's caused them to consider selling their horses, or the hope that they'll just be able to improve their horsemanship in some way. Everyone we see has some sort of hope that they would like to realize someday.

When Mark welcomes the students as they enter the arena to do their session, he asks them what *they* would like to work on. At the summer clinics, he asks each student to articulate his or her goals for the week. I think what he's really asking those students is what their hopes are, what they wish for. Then he helps them toward fulfilling those hopes and wishes in whatever way he can.

I was helping a woman on a young horse in Illinois in November, and as we were working on settling her horse down, she said, "I hope someday my horse will be able to just stand there like yours does." Her hope was a simple one, but it meant a lot to her. If we dare have them, our hopes are important to us. They're so important to us that sometimes it's scary to give voice to them.

And really, if we have a passion for horses, that passion is often a combination of love and hope and fear and awe. It's all in there, and that's what makes the horse so magical to us. I wonder sometimes if the horses have hopes for us as well.

⸺⬥⸺

Working for Mark was my own private crucible in a lot of ways. I couldn't know in what ways I would change and grow and evolve during my apprenticeship because I'd never done anything like that before. The job itself shapes you, and the horses shape you, and then there are all the choices we make that define who we are and what we're about.

One of the biggest changes I've seen in myself during my apprenticeship with Mark is that I've opened up some. I hadn't really noticed, but in my adulthood, I'd become shy, reticent—almost withdrawn. I was pretty closed when it came to anything outside my comfort zone. It was hard for me to go anywhere new or try things I'd never tried before.

It was in horsemanship that I was first willing to open up and experiment with some new things and get out of my box. I'm still in the process of doing that, because old teachings and habits truly die hard. I still find myself pulling ideas and techniques out of my tool kit that I'm not sure are based on a true understanding of how horses work. I won't throw that stuff out, but I'll evaluate it as it comes up and take a fresh look at it based on what I believe to be true about horses now.

When I began to open up a bit in my horsemanship, it necessitated that I begin to do the same in my life as well, and working as Mark's apprentice certainly gave me opportunities to do that. Every week, I met new people with unique histories, goals, and experiences. Each person I met challenged me to open myself up to what they could show me about themselves, about myself, and about the world around us. I got a lot of practice at simply meeting people and having conversations, which is something I hadn't practiced much before. I've become more comfortable with other people; I've become more comfortable with myself.

I didn't have many friends when I began my apprenticeship with Mark, and now I have quite a few. They're good friends that I'll probably have for life. I didn't foresee friendships as a possible benefit of working for Mark, but it certainly has been. I think Mark and I have become pretty good friends, too, and I believe we'll remain so.

Aikido was something that took me completely out of my comfort zone. I sure couldn't have gone to my first aikido class a year-and-a-half ago. I don't think I'd have seen the benefit at the time, and I certainly wouldn't have had the courage. Aikido has shown me how generous people can be with their time, their knowledge, and their bodies and how it's possible for me to do things physically that I didn't believe were feasible. I see that the dojo isn't just a place; it's something we can take with us if we wish. The arena can be our dojo, the freeway can be our dojo, heck, life can be our dojo, if we choose to look at it that way.

I think I've also become open to the future. I do not know just what the future will hold, and that's okay. I know that it will hold horses and hard work, and that's all I need to know. The future's not scary if we choose not to be frightened by it. The hope and belief that things will work out is something tangible when not much else is. And things will change. If we do nothing but wait, things around us will shift, and I bet the direction we're to follow will become clear. One way or another, I'll end up just where I'm supposed to be, when I'm supposed to be there.

━━◈━━

For the year I worked with Mark, I joined a subculture, a brotherhood of mostly men who travel the country and the world working with horses by giving clinics. In April, as we drove to spend the night with clinician Harry Whitney at his place in Arizona on our way to San Diego, we passed Buck Brannaman heading north as we headed south through the desert. In November, as we headed home from Illinois, we were on an overpass as a Parelli convoy passed underneath us. At any one time, all over the world, these guys are crisscrossing back and forth ceaselessly, going where the work takes them.

I like the life. I like the travel and meeting new people and horses. I like the idea of helping people for a while, and then turning their horsemanship back over to them. If I'm lucky, I'll get to go back later and see what they've done since I saw them last. I like having the opportunity to discuss horsemanship *ad nauseum*. And most of all, I like having horses around me all the time, where I can watch them, smell them, touch them, and learn from them.

Horses themselves embody hope in a lot of ways. They begin every day hoping for the best, even if yesterday didn't turn out very well for them. It seems like they're just naturally optimistic. When we're working with them, I think we should try to leave them the way they're made—cheerful, sensitive, powerful, and gorgeous. Horses have a peace about them. Just having them around shows us that peace and hope are possible in our own lives.

If we can preserve those things in the horse, maybe we can find them in ourselves. That's my hope, anyway.